TRADITIONAL
QUILTING

Part Author of

RURAL INDUSTRIES OF ENGLAND AND WALES

VOLUMES I—III

1   Quilt made in 1939 by Mrs. Coulthard, Weardale, with
feather twist border

TRADITIONAL QUILTING

Its Story and its Practice

By
MAVIS
FITZRANDOLPH

London
B. T. BATSFORD LTD

First Published 1954

MADE AND PRINTED IN GREAT BRITAIN BY
WILLIAM CLOWES AND SONS, LIMITED, LONDON AND BECCLES
FOR THE PUBLISHERS
B. T. BATSFORD LTD
4 FITZHARDINGE STREET, PORTMAN SQUARE
LONDON, W.1

PREFACE

THE object of this book is to put on record as much of the traditional lore about quilting as I have been able to collect. Many old quilters have died in the last forty years or so without leaving anyone of a younger generation who will continue to use their frames; thus many threads of tradition have been broken off short and it seems worth while to pick up the ends of those which have been carried down to the present and, by weaving them together, to form a picture of this ancient and interesting craft. Much has been written about American quilts (though more about the patchwork which is usually combined with quilting in that country); little has been written about British quilting and I believe that Mrs. Hake[1] is the only writer who has previously carried out any searching enquiry, as she did in the south-west of England with unexpectedly rich results.

During the years 1920–23 a survey of rural industries was carried out in every county of England and Wales under the direction of the Agricultural Economics Research Institute, Oxford, but in the volume of the published reports[2] dealing with Wales there is no mention of quilting, whilst in another volume it is referred to only very briefly as a home craft in the north of England, with a passing reference to the fact that quilts were sometimes made for sale. Yet at the time when that survey was made there were certainly dozens of village quilters at work for their livelihood and perhaps hundreds of quilt clubs in profitable action. They were so little known beyond the circles of their local customers that none of the authorities whom the investigators consulted in each county thought them worth mentioning if, indeed, they knew of them.

During the last twenty-five years (but with a gap of nearly ten years from 1940) I have been in touch with quilters in South Wales,

1 *English Quilting Old and New*, by Elizabeth Hake. Batsford, 1937.
2 *The Rural Industries of England and Wales*, vols. I–III (England), by Helen E. FitzRandolph and M. Doriel Hay; vol. IV (Wales), by Anna M. Jones. Clarendon Press, 1916–27.

County Durham and Northumberland, and from the first I have been interested in the traditional lore of their craft, though up to 1939 I was chiefly concerned with organizing the sale of their work. All the notes which I had made before that date were destroyed when the offices of the Rural Institutes Bureau were damaged in the London blitz, but much remained in my memory and in 1948 it was suggested by Mr. D. L. Jones, O.B E., secretary of Monmouthshire Rural Community Council, and by Dr Iowerth Peate, M.A., D.Sc., F.S.A., Keeper in Charge of the Welsh Folk Museum in St. Fagan's Castle, that all available information about Welsh traditional quilting ought to be collected and put on record. The Rural Industries Bureau undertook to finance the investigation and at a later stage Mr. Cosmo Clark, its Director, decided that my survey should be extended to the north of England—an idea which I welcomed as enabling me to give a more complete picture of the industry. In the course of my investigation I have been in touch with over one hundred and fifty quilters, most of whom I have talked to. Mr. D. L. Jones, who has given me much help, made contact with many Welsh quilters by means of broadcasts, letters to the local press and conferences, and sent out many questionaries which produced some information on basic facts and suggested lines for the start of my enquiry. The exhibition of old and new quilts which was organized by Mr. Jones and the Welsh Folk Museum at St. Fagan's Castle in July 1951 provided me with the opportunity to study a quantity of the best work of today side by side with many fine old quilts. But my information has been collected chiefly in conversation with quilters and owners of old quilts, with some correspondence to clear up doubtful points. Quilters, like other traditional craftsmen, often dogmatize, each one tending to recognize only her own way as the right way. Therefore a representative picture can only be composed after prolonged enquiry. I have tried to put on record as much variety of opinion as possible, but in Chapter Four I have, for the sake of clarity in describing the way in which a quilt is made, concentrated on the technique of one particular worker.

My information about quilting in the United States has been gathered from three books: Marie D. Webster, in *Quilts—Their Story and How to Make Them* (Tudor Publishing Co., New York, 1915) ranges over many subjects and is interested mainly in patchwork and very little in quilting. Ruth E. Finley, in *Old Patchwork Quilts and the Women Who Made Them*, also assumes that anything called a quilt is made of patchwork and does not pay much attention to the patterns or technique of quilting. Florence Peto, in *American Quilts and Coverlets* (Max Parrish & Co., Ltd., 1949) gives an interesting chronological account of quilts and coverlets of many varieties and recognizes quilting as a craft in its own right.

It is not easy to study traditional quilting today except by visiting the workers themselves and other local people who still cherish old quilts. The Victoria and Albert Museum has a considerable number of quilted garments, and some quilts, of English seventeenth- and eighteenth-century workmanship, and although very few of these may be on view at any given time they can all be examined by anyone interested who writes to the Textiles Department of the Museum to make an appointment. The Welsh Folk Museum has some Welsh work and there are a few pieces, I believe, scattered amongst the provincial museums. There is a charming miniature Queen Anne quilt on a doll's bed in Parham House, an Elizabethan house in Sussex which is open to the public on certain days, and there may be quilts on view in other great houses. But nearly all such specimens which I have seen are of the grander kind; the cottage or farmhouse quilt was not thought worthy of preservation, although probably it would be more interesting to us today in showing the trend of tradition through the ages. I think this book will serve a useful purpose if it only encourages owners to cherish even their humblest old quilts and, if a time comes when no member of the family cares to preserve them, to offer them to museums, together with any appurtenances of the craft, such as frames (particularly any of unusual type) and templates, especially the more durable sort of wood or tin.

I am indebted to a great many people for help in compiling the material for this book. Without the backing of the Rural Industries Bureau I could not have collected the information; various members of its staff, as well as Rural Industries organizers in the provinces, have helped in several ways, Mr. J. N. White, the Bureau's Information Officer, in particular; Mr. Victor Schafer deserves special mention for his work in photographing the quilts (always difficult subjects) and especially for the series of pictures of a quilter at work which show the technique of quilting in a way which has not, I think, been attempted before. Mrs. F. M. Fletcher, who cheerfully endured considerable discomfort as the subject (or perhaps I should say the victim) of this sequence, has also earned my deep gratitude for the immense amount of help she has given me by answering my questions, seeking out interesting quilts for me to see, lending her drawings of templates and patterns (on which the diagrams on pages 79, 80, 81, 117 and 119 are based) and reading Chapter Four. Mrs. Gordon Hake, Miss Muriel Rose, Miss Helen FitzRandolph (who supplied the information in Appendix II about agricultural labourers' earnings), Mr. W. E. Rains (who answered my enquiries about the manufacture of cotton-wool and wadding), all deserve my thanks for their help. Finally I acknowledge with much gratitude the kindness of all those who in various ways helped me to find and examine old quilts (especially the Cumberland, Northumberland and Westmorland Federations of Women's Institutes), and the great number of quilters and quilt owners who cheerfully gave their time and ransacked their stores to share their knowledge with me and to show me their work and, in many cases, lent precious quilts to be photographed. They are too many to be named here, and every one of them has contributed something to this book.

Slinfold, Sussex   M. FitzRandolph
       1953

ACKNOWLEDGMENT

THE Author and Publishers would like to thank the following for permission to reproduce the photographs included in this book: The British Council, for fig. 45; *The Farmers' Weekly*, for fig. 17; The National Museum of Wales, Welsh Folk Museum, for fig. 9; Miss Muriel Rose, for fig. 4; the Rural Industries Bureau, for figs. 1, 3, 5, 6, 11-15, 18-44, 46, 48-51, 53-5 and 57; Mrs. Thompson, for fig. 7; the Trustees of the Victoria and Albert Museum, for figs. 2, 10 and 52; Watson's Studios, Aberdare, for fig. 16.

CONTENTS

LIST OF ILLUSTRATIONS

HALF-TONE PLATES

LINE ILLUSTRATIONS IN THE TEXT

CHAPTER ONE

The Background

"HOW now, blown Jack? how now, quilt?" says the Prince to Falstaff in *Henry IV* (Part I, Act IV, sc. ii) —showing that, when Shakespeare wrote, the padded quilt was a natural homely image for a fat man. By about 1900 the phrase, if it meant anything to most readers of Shakespeare, would have suggested an eiderdown—an object which Shakespeare certainly did not know in anything like its present form.

"A bed-cover of two cloths sewed together with something soft between them" is the definition of a quilt in *Chambers's Twentieth Century Dictionary*, and that is the sense in which the term is used in this book. The bald definition does not suggest that quilts are a promising subject. But quilting is one of the few handicrafts, and the only needlework, still carried on in this country which embodies an unbroken tradition stretching back to an obscure origin in the distant past. Moreover, the words "sewed together" are important; the lines of stitching, which hold together the two pieces of material and the soft padding between, form patterns, and it is these which give the traditional quilts their characteristic beauty and interest.

Information about the history of quilting is scanty. The *Encyclopædia Britannica* (11th edition) tells us that the word "quilt" came into English from the Old French *cuilte*, which was derived from the Latin *culcita* or *culcitra*, meaning a stuffed mattress or cushion. Also the Low Latin *culcita puncta*, a stitched or quilted cushion (probably a form of quilt), became through a series of changes *counterpane*, which has now lost its sense of something padded. Although the earliest form of quilt may have been a warm coverlet, quilting was also used a great deal in body armour.[1] The Norman hawberk might be of chain mail or "of thick cotton and old linen *padded and quilted* in lozenges, squares or lines". In the thirteenth century "the knight's hawberk is worn over a gambeson of linen, *quilted linen* or cotton, which lesser men wear with a steel cap for all defence." The fourteenth-century knight seems to have been particularly well padded, for he wore a haketon of some soft material, over this a hawberk of mail, over the hawberk a leather garment, and over this again a sleeveless gambeson or pourpoint of leather or *quilted work*, studded and enriched. Chaucer's Sir Thopas, in the latter half of this century, wore a *quilted haketon* next his shirt, and over that the habergeon, a lesser hawberk of chain mail. Froissart mentions a knight whose haketon, worn under his coat of mail, was "stuffed with twisted silk." In fact a quilted garment of some sort was evidently an essential part of a suit of armour, though it might be worn either under or over the mail, and it was also a satisfactory substitute for the mail. "The fully armed man was always a rare figure in war . . . the country gentleman, serving as light horseman or mounted archer, would hold himself well armed had he a quilted jack or brigandine and a basinet or salet."

We think of armour as metal plates or rings because those were the more durable parts of it which have outlasted their use and can be seen in many collections today. The quilted gambesons, pourpoints, haketons and jacks, of perishable materials, have long since crumbled to dust. The knight returned from the wars may have found that his quilted haketon had its peace-time uses in his draughty castle in winter, and perhaps he wore it until the padding came out at the elbows and his wife threw it away. We do not know whether the quilter of those days exercised his or her ingenuity in something more elaborate than "lozenges, squares or lines," but probably the padding was thick and so no fine stitching would be possible.

Much of what we know about quilting since the days of armour can be found in *Notes on Quilting* issued by the Victoria

[1] See article "Arms and Armour," *Ency. Brit.*, 11th ed.

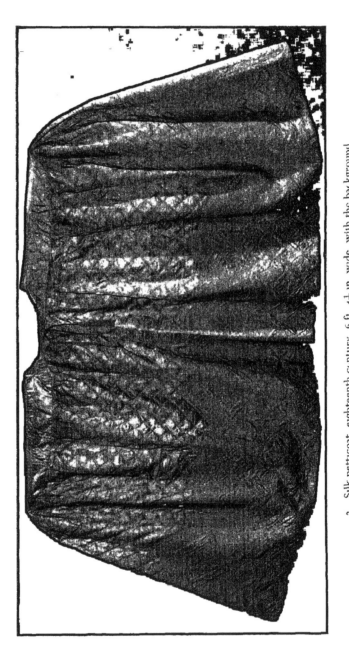

2   Silk petticoat, eighteenth century, 6 ft 4½ in wide, with the background of the lower part quilted with very close lines   All in running stitch

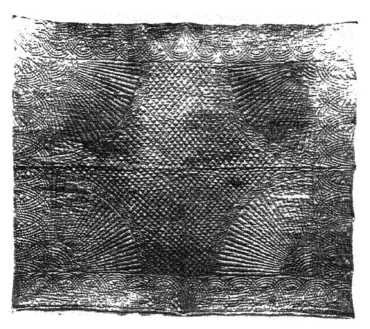

3 Eighteenth-century farmhouse quilt of woollen homespun, owned by Mrs. Snaith, Netherton, Northumberland

4 Cot quilt in sea-waves pattern made by the Merthyr Group, South Wales, in the 1930's

and Albert Museum, but this writer, in common with others, does not always distinguish between the form of quilt which is still traditional in Britain—a textile sandwich in which the lines of stitching hold the filling in place between the two layers of material—and other forms which are padded only in parts or even, in some cases, not padded at all. The Sicilian quilt made about 1400, illustrated in the frontispiece to the Museum booklet and often mentioned as the earliest known quilt, is a purely decorative piece of work in which only the design is padded so that it stands up in relief against a flat background. Many other pieces of work illustrated in this booklet are made with a similar technique, the design—outlined usually in backstitch—being stuffed with little wads of wool or with a very loosely spun two-ply woollen thread, sometimes used double or treble. The statement that "the stitching is usually done in backstitch" applies to this work but not to the traditional wadded quilting, in which running stitch was generally used in the past, as it is today.

This "stuffing" technique was sometimes combined with that more usual at the present day in which the padding is first laid in smoothly between the two layers of material and then quilted through. A beautiful eighteenth-century underskirt in the Victoria and Albert Museum has its upper part worked in flat wadded quilting in a diamond pattern and the elaborate design of its lower part stuffed. Possibly these two methods of work were often combined to produce something rather grander than the ordinary flat wadded quilting. Certainly they were used together in America until the early nineteenth century. Marie Webster[1] describes some old American white quilts in which "the design is further accentuated by having all the most prominent features, such as the leaves and petals of flowers, stuffed. To accomplish this tiny holes are made on the wrong side of each section of the design and cotton (wadding) is pushed in with a large needle until the section is stuffed full and tight. This tedious process is followed until every leaf and petal stands

[1] *Quilts—Their Story and How to Make Them*, by Marie D. Webster. Tudor Publishing Co , New York, 1915.

19

out in bold relief." Florence Peto[1] illustrates and describes what she calls a "corded spread" in which the whole background is stuffed with candlewick inserted from the back between parallel lines of sewing, whilst the design, in eighteenth-century style with flowing leaf, fruit and flower shapes, is all stuffed from the back with wads of cotton. This was made on Long Island in 1830–31.

Although the forms of quilting in which the padding is only used for decorative effect and not for warmth were done in England for some hundreds of years, they do not survive as traditional crafts, nor have I found amongst the quilts still preserved in private homes any instance of this additional stuffing of a wadded quilt. These techniques were practised for the adornment of fine houses or of fine ladies and gentlemen. Wadded quilting, although utilitarian in origin, was not restricted to padding the man-of-war and keeping the cottager warm. It was used from medieval times to adorn rich hangings and bed coverlets and, in the seventeenth and eighteenth centuries, quilted coats, waistcoats and doublets, dresses and petticoats were fashionable. Household inventories and other lists of goods from the fifteenth to the eighteenth centuries (see Appendix I) mention quilts; in the latter period they are of calico or linen as well as silk and may be backed with lindsey (a mixture of wool and flax) or lutestring (a kind of glossy silk). The multitude of quilts which must have been made and used in humbler homes throughout this period have no written record and never found their way into museums.

Although this book is about *quilts* in the strict sense of the term, inevitably patchwork and applied work come into the story because they were so much used by the traditional quilters. Mosaic patchwork, in which small pieces of material cut to geometric shapes are joined together, seems to have been made first in the eighteenth century and to have been used mainly, then and since, for the top covers of quilted coverlets.[2]

---

[1] *American Quilts and Coverlets*, by Florence Peto. Max Parrish and Co. Ltd., 1949. (Chanticleer Press Inc., New York.)

[2] See *Notes on Quilting* and *Notes on Applied Work and Patchwork*. Victoria and Albert Museum, 1932 and 1938; reprinted 1949.

No earlier examples of this kind of work are known, and it really bears no relation to the applied work of earlier centuries, generally ecclesiastical. In America too this "pieced work" as it is called there, seems to have come into existence, without any forerunners, at about the same time. Ruth Finley[1] says that the oldest surviving pieced quilts were made between 1775 and 1800, and although "quilts" are mentioned earlier, in inventories from 1692 and in advertisements of sales of household goods in 1727 and 1729, these are not necessarily of pieced work[2]. "White quilts" (that is to say, made of uncut material) are also known in America, but the making of mosaic patchwork and also of applied work (known in the States, quite logically, as "patched work" or patchwork) became so popular among the American colonists, and their elaborate designs are so famous, that American writers are apt to assume that the mention of a "quilt" implies pieced or applied work. Certainly the early settlers took their quilting frames and pattern templates with them, for quilted petticoats were worn by women in the colonial days and they had quilted curtains as well as bed-covers in their houses. Whether mosaic patchwork was first added to quilting in this country or in America, or whether it sprang into existence on both sides of the Atlantic simultaneously, it is impossible to decide. I like to think that it was invented here and that someone, hearing of the bitter winters and hard living conditions which her emigrated relatives had to endure, decided to send them a warm quilt and, moreover, to give it a gay top cover in this new style, which was much admired and eagerly imitated in the new country. But this is mere conjecture.

Marie Webster says that only the English and Dutch settlers quilted, and Ruth Finley adds that the Pennsylvania Dutch quilts are "superlative" in quilting. The former believes that quilting, and the patchwork that came to be associated with it, developed so abundantly and have survived so extensively in the United States because of the lonely lives of the pioneer women

1 See *Old Patchwork Quilts and the Women Who Made Them*, by Ruth E. Finley. Lippincott; Philadelphia and London, 1929.
2 *Quilts—Their Story and How to Make Them*, by Marie D. Webster.

and their need to be self-sufficing. The "quilting bees," when neighbours were invited to come and work at the quilting frame, after the patchwork was done, also provided welcome social occasions, and the work met a need for self-expression and for gay decoration in the house. Ruth Finley gives the further information that in the early pioneer days textiles were precious, nearly all being imported, blankets were not in general use and the houses were inadequately heated. These three factors helped to popularize quilts, and especially those with one or two covers of patchwork which made use of every spare scrap of material.

In this country, patchwork quilts made in the eighteenth century, or the early years of the nineteenth, are occasionally found (11), but probably most of them have been worn out. Certainly many were made later; when any North Country woman of a farming family shows you her collection of quilts made by her mother and grandmother, and even perhaps her great grandmother (that is to say they date usually from about 1850 to 1910), you are sure to find patchwork amongst them; in fact the patched quilts will probably outnumber the plain ones. The same is true of South Wales, though here the patchwork is generally of a cruder kind.

Towards the close of the eighteenth century quilted clothing ceased to be fashionable and even the bed quilt gradually went out of use in most parts of Britain during the nineteenth century, as factory-made bed-covers of various kinds became cheaper and more plentiful. In particular the "marcella" quilt, machine-woven of white cotton with a raised design to imitate the effect of quilting, although it had not the warmth of a wadded quilt, probably did much to drive the hand-stitched quilt out of fashion at a time when "machine-made" implied novelty and smartness.

As the hand-stitched quilt became less common the word "quilt" began to be used for other kinds of coverlet. Patchwork covers in particular, because so many of them were actually padded and stitched in a frame, were often spoken of as "patchwork quilts" even when they were not quilted. The tremendous popularity of patchwork in New England has caused the word "quilt" there to become almost synonymous with "patchwork" or "pieced work."

The meaning of the word "quilt" has been still further confused by some writers on embroidery who have used it to mean any kind of bed covering which is decorated with needle-work; thus an "embroidered quilt" may be a counterpane embroidered on a single piece of material, having no connection whatever with the craft of quilting. The designation "eider-down quilt" draws yet another red herring across the trail. This, it is true, is a padded bed-cover but the technique of making it is quite different from that of quilting; the down cannot be treated in the same way as wool or cotton wadding because it would work its way out through holes made by the needle—apart from the fact that its fluffy nature, in contrast to the fairly compact mass of the paddings used in quilts, would make it difficult, if not impossible, to stitch through.

The evidence indicates that in the nineteenth century traditional quilting, ignored by the world of fashion, yet held its own in the cottages and farmhouses of England and Wales; but by about the middle of the century it was going out of use in many parts of the country although in some districts it was still practised, in communities which were isolated and not within easy reach of the shops where the novel factory goods were to be seen, and by people who were poor and must therefore be thrifty. In South Wales and the northern counties of England it has persisted up to the present day. Possibly quilters could still be found in Scotland; I know of at least one old quilt of Scottish origin and have heard of a few quilters still at work there within recent years, and the general conditions would seem to be of the kind in which quilting was likely to persist.

Mrs. Hake, in her book *English Quilting Old and New* (Batsford, 1937), told how her researches showed that traditional quilting was still widely done in south-western England up to about fifty years ago and similar enquiries might bring evidence to light in other parts of the country. In mid-Wales it was prac-tised in many homes until sixty years ago, and some made it their living, according to a correspondent, ninety years old, of Rhayader (Rads.).

But the evidence must be sought soon if it is to be found; quilts which have fulfilled their comforting purpose for more than fifty years have come to a thin and tattered state. "It's gettin' a long way on its journey," said an old lady apologetically as she displayed one such relic, with the padding showing through its worn covering. Moreover, since quilting came down in the world in the nineteenth century and thereafter had little prestige as handicraft until interest in it was revived in the last thirty years or so, the old quilts have not always been cherished by the younger generation. Mrs. Snaith (Northumberland) rescued from amongst the belongings of a neighbour who died at the age of ninety, a piece of exquisitely quilted blue silk, two hundred years old and probably intended originally for an underskirt (6); it had been roughly hacked into two strips, pieces had been cut out of it and it would have been thrown away by the old lady's relatives. Too often have old quilts been used as underlays beneath mattresses and thus been ruined by rust from the bed springs. In South Wales a panel from one of the quilted silk petticoats which were made in such numbers in the late nineteenth century and are now so hard to find was given to a church guild to be made into a banner! The rest, being motheaten, was thrown away. A quilter will appreciate and value the work of past generations, but her daughters, if they have never learnt the craft, will discard it as old-fashioned stuff.

The provincial museums could do much to preserve valuable evidence of this fine traditional handicraft and might save from destruction not only quilts but also frames and pattern templates which come by inheritance into the hands of those no longer interested in them. The National Museum of Wales preserves in its Folk Department at St. Fagan's Castle not only old quilts but also some good modern specimens, and did much to stimulate local appreciation of the craft by its exhibition, in the summer of 1951, of ancient and modern Welsh quilting.

Doubtless the utilitarian qualities of quilting, its home-made warmth, helped to keep it alive. Many accounts of the materials used fifty years ago and more—patchwork of tailors' and dressmakers' pieces, and rag padding, for instance—show that in many homes it was essentially a thrift craft. But the humble

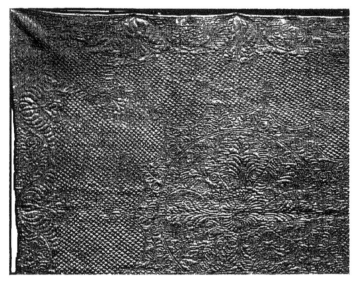

5   Part of a wedding quilt made in Weardale about 1911 by Miss Humble
Owned by Mrs M E Milburn

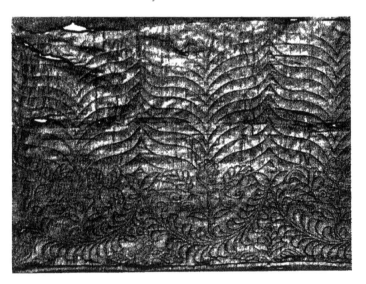

6   Pieces of quilted blue silk, mid-eighteenth century, probably intended
for a petticoat.   Owned by Mrs. Snaith, Northumberland

7   Mussel gatherers at Runswick about 1870, some wearing quilted skirts

8   An unusual type of quilting frame from Weardale, with ratchets.
Owned by Mrs Graham Peart

craftswomen doubtless found the same satisfaction in creating and stitching their lovely patterns as any other artist finds in his work. As well as bed quilts and cradle covers, they quilted petticoats, which Welsh countrywomen, fishermen's wives on the north-east coast (7) and Northumberland bondagers[1] continued to wear in stiff, ample folds. Although quilts of the heavier kinds of "thrift" materials (which were particularly popular in Wales) were, necessarily, coarsely worked, finer work was still done when better materials could be afforded; the framed certificates to be seen on cottage walls in Wales, recording awards for quilting at the Welsh industries exhibitions held in London in 1903 and 1904, and at the International Exhibition at the White City in 1911 (and probably others), indicate that even the wider, commercialized world did then—perhaps through the influence of the Arts and Crafts movement —recognize quilting as a fine handicraft, though little interest seems to have been taken in it generally. But a few discerning women began to notice the beautiful work which was done so unpretentiously and thought so little of. Amongst others, Miss Alice Armes in County Durham and Lady Lisburne in Southwest Wales took pains to bring quilting to more general notice and to encourage the quilters.

During the last thirty years a quantity of traditional quilted work has appeared in handicraft exhibitions and much has been written about it, but little research has been done to trace its history back through the dark ages of the last hundred and fifty years to the time when it disappeared from the fashionable world. This book is an attempt to fill that gap and although it can at this date be filled only with scattered and sketchy pictures, these do throw some light upon the social history of our countryside.

[1] Bondager—a woman field worker in the Border country.

CHAPTER TWO

The Quilters

THERE are many quilters living today who learnt their craft towards the end of the nineteenth or at the beginning of the twentieth century, and from what they have told me, and from examination of the quilts made by them and by their forebears (generally on the distaff side, though there are men, too, in the story), I have pieced together a picture of the home craft of quilting as it was carried on during the past hundred and fifty years in the countryside of South Wales and the north of England. Here women worked at the quilt frame in many farmhouses and cottages, and in a few of the great houses (though in some cases only in the kitchen or servants' hall). Many families in Wales, like that of Mrs. Bowen whose people came from Pembrokeshire to Mountain Ash, "looked on a quilting frame as part of the home." "Quilts were part of our lives," said another, "like tables and chairs." Mr. George Davies, the son of a Pembrokeshire quilter, described a childhood memory probably shared by hundreds when he wrote: "I have the make of the frame and my mother sitting there, hour after hour, very vivid in my mind."

In the north of England they were *twilts* and many of the older generation still use this pleasant word and speak also of the *pattrons* on them, though with the spread of standardized pronunciation these forms are dying out.

In Westmorland I have been told that there were quilts in all the farmhouses in the old days. "A lot of quilting was done on the farms in the winter," said Mrs. Robinson; they reckoned to make a rag mat and so many quilts each year—she herself made fifteen one winter, being in need of them for the farm hands and having a maid who was keen on the work. In Cumberland, too, you would find them in every farmhouse, several on a bed. In Northumberland in the old days "everyone quilted," and most country families still own quilts, though some do not use them much now because they are so heavy to wash. Throughout County Durham there are many old quilts to be found, particularly in Weardale. The point of view of those "old days" so often referred to was expressed by an elderly lady here who, after visiting a neighbour who was ill in bed, exclaimed in shocked surprise: "Not one twilt did she have!"

For many little girls the sight of mother sitting at her quilting frame might mean that they had a task which would keep them from their play—they must thread a number of needles and stick them in a corner of the quilt ready for use. Several Welshwomen recalled that this always had to be done as soon as they got home from school; a Durham woman used to thread needles for an old Yorkshire quilter (born on the same day as Queen Victoria) at Guisborough, where she lived as a girl; but for Mrs. Hitchcock (Co. Durham) this task was a treat, for she was allowed to leave her lessons twice a week to thread needles for a group of quilters who worked to raise funds for the Methodist Chapel. "Round and round I went, sticking the needles in their little pin-cushions."

Stories of the old quilters show how work at the frame might be a regular part of the farm routine. Miss Humble of Weardale, who quilted and marked the patterns on quilts for a living, was never in bed after five in the morning; the farm work was done by nine and then she quilted till noon. After dinner there were the calves to feed, and other farm jobs. A big quilt with elaborate pattern took Mrs. J. E. Peart, working together with her mother and aunt, six weeks to make in the time spared from farm work. Miss Humble never quilted by lamplight, but others of that hardy race, like a farmer's wife near Bellingham in Northumberland, worked by candlelight. Quilting and mat-making was all they had to do in the long winter evenings. When this old lady died she left "a mass of quilts," some plain and some patched, which were divided among the family; one of her descendants thought she might have some stored away but had none in use. The Misses Johnson in Hexhamshire have two glass globes for magnifying candlelight to quilt by, like those which were used by Buckinghamshire lacemakers. The candles themselves were made at home—"candle-making day was Grannie's delight."

A Welshwoman recalled how her mother would say one day: "We'll start a quilt tomorrow at nine and we'll work on it till four," and so they did. As soon as father had gone to work the essential chores were hurriedly done and then the frame was set up; mother and daughter worked steadily till four and then put the frame aside in time to get tea ready for father, who came home at five. "If we hadn't kept to mother's plan we should never have got a quilt done; we were always so busy." I think this gives the answer to those who now say that there was more quilting done in the old days because people had more time and weren't so busy as we are now. In fact they were probably busier, because fewer necessities could be bought ready-made and many more tasks had to be done by hand in the kitchen and household; shops were fewer, and far distant from many country homes, with no buses by which to reach them quickly. But making quilts was as necessary as making bread, and therefore time had to be found for it.

These statements about quilting in "the old days" (roughly 1880 to 1910) refer generally to the countryside rather than to the towns. But the craft was brought into the mining districts of South Wales and of County Durham from the rural areas. Many quilters in the Rhondda and Aberdare and Merthyr have told me that their families came from Carmarthenshire or Pembrokeshire; to the Durham mines families migrated from Teesdale and Weardale and from Cleveland (Yorkshire); a Northumberland mining village remembers that a trainload of Devonshire people brought up to break a strike included wives who brought their quilt frames. Mrs. Lace of Aberdare uses a frame which was made in Scotland early in the nineteenth century and was brought down to Wales by her grandfather, who, returning to his birthplace there after the death of his parents, selected only this and an oak bureau to take home with him.

Towards the end of the nineteenth century probably the majority of quilters in the North Country, and a great many in South Wales, were what I will call HOME QUILTERS; that is to say, they made quilts only for their own families, not for a living. Quilting was a family affair; often mother and grannie, or mother and an aunt, worked together at the frame, and the daughters would learn, as soon as they were old enough to sew, often at fourteen, by helping their mother at the frame. Mrs. Isabella Fletcher (Co. Durham) learnt when she was eleven, from "the old lady" in the house in which she was nursemaid, who was quilting stays for the children, and who also quilted petticoats for herself. Mrs. Ritson also learnt at eleven, from her elder sister. Mrs. Hick's mother, a Nottinghamshire woman, only learnt to quilt when she came to live in County Durham; when her older children had all gone out to work she started the youngest girl at the frame to keep her at home. Another woman remembers how as a small girl she was rapped over the knuckles by her mother when she "didn't do it right." One or two others "learnt rough" from their mothers—doubtless to work on household quilts—and later learned finer work and a greater variety of patterns from professional quilters.

In a certain Carmarthenshire family, when mother came home with a new idea for a quilt pattern, father would clear the floor and chalk the pattern, according to her instructions, on the stone flags. When work was started on the quilt, the daughters all helped with the sewing. This was not the only man who played his part in the quilting. In the north of England, where more permanent templates for pattern-marking are found, these were often cut from plywood, or even tin, by the menfolk, who sometimes produced new shapes from their own ideas. Mrs. William Hodgson's husband always kept a supply of needles threaded for her when she was quilting regularly under the Rural Industries Bureau's scheme (Chapter Three) and he "holds the stick" (criticizes). Mrs. Reaveley told me how, in her youth, at Jarrow on Tyne, when a group of women were making quilts for the chapel funds, the menfolk would come and thread needles for them. Then they had refreshments for all and made a party of it. Unemployed husbands did the washing up when their wives were busy on quilts, because when your hands are softened by being much in water they more easily become sore from needle pricks. It was an unemployed Welsh miner who asked me once if I remembered the corner pattern on his wife's last quilt; "Rose and leaves it was; well, I worked one of those corners myself." Very proud of it he was.

"The girls of the family all helped in making quilts," said a Welshwoman, "and as each was married she had all the quilts she needed." They were an important part of a girl's dowry; six seems to have been the usual allowance in Wales. In Westmorland and Cumberland quilts were always made for a girl's wedding, and in the latter county sometimes for the young man too if he came of a farming family. A Welsh itinerant quilter said she had made marriage quilts for men, and once she made half a dozen quilts for a lad who was going away to a job in the Midlands; evidently his mother was determined that he should have his home comforts in that distant place.

Many marriage quilts were shown to me in Northumberland and County Durham, but here it seemed to be the custom for just one very handsome quilt to be made by a woman for her daughter's wedding. They do not seem to have been made anywhere in this country in such quantities as in America where, Ruth Finley tells us, a bride's dower chest in the old days should contain a dozen ordinary quilts as well as the "bride's quilt" which was only made when she became engaged.

A Northumberland quilter made one for her older daughter, but the younger one, a few years later, scorned the idea "because quilting had gone out then" (about 1920–30). A girl in County Durham turned down the offer of a marriage quilt at about the same time but regretted it when she read in a newspaper soon afterwards that Welsh and Durham quilts were being made for one of London's most expensive hotels.

Making marriage quilts for her daughters and sometimes for her sons, cradle quilts for the new generation, and workaday quilts to keep all members of the household snug at nights, must have kept the housewife busy, and she was glad of help from anyone in the family who could sew well, and even from neighbours, who were sometimes invited in to help. "And so the party went from house to house," said one Welsh informant, and others, both in Wales and Northumberland, also told how several neighbours—sometimes four or five—would work together at the frame, making a quilt for each of them in turn. The quilts so made would be only for home use; the professional quilter, whose work was her livelihood, frowned on this communal quilting. As Mrs. Thomas (Aberdare) said: "The making of a quilt was regarded as a craft. The craftswoman would start and finish the job herself; it was something in which any casual caller was not allowed to interfere. When two worked at one frame it was a case of one craftswoman and an apprentice, who spent two years before she served her time." Mrs. Armstrong, a very fine Northumberland quilter, also said that although she had been asked to work with neighbours at the frame it was a thing she never liked doing.

Mrs. Bowen (from a Pembrokeshire family) told how her mother made her first quilt in 1873 at Clynderwen, in the home of the Gower family where she was chambermaid. It was a big household, with twenty-two servants, and when the dressmaker paid her annual visit and stayed for some weeks, making ball dresses and other gowns for the ladies, all the cuttings were saved and given to the maids to make into patchwork. When a "facing" was complete the maker was given a piece of print for the backing and then it was set up in the frame and quilted. Mrs. Bowen still has the quilt made by her mother in this way, of silk "patches" in rich and gay colours, with a Paisley-style print on the reverse side. "The old lady," she said, "didn't like the maids to go out at night and so encouraged them to stay in and work at their quilts."

The *professional quilters* I will classify as (1) VILLAGE QUILTERS, of whom there were many throughout South Wales and some in the North Country, and with them I include the North Country pattern-markers; (2) ITINERANT QUILTERS, seldom heard of outside South Wales, and (3) women who ran QUILT CLUBS, which were a feature of the mining districts in both areas.

33

(1) VILLAGE QUILTERS. A certain Mary Jones of Panteg near Llanarth (Cardiganshire), commonly known as "Mari Panteg," who died about 1900, seems to have been one of the most famous of Welsh village quilters and is perhaps typical of them all. Many people in that district still treasure her quilts; she had orders for miles around, particularly from girls about to be married. She lived in a primitive little stone cottage of one storey and worked by the light of a tiny single-paned window. One of her quilts which I have seen, made about 1850 when she was a young woman, is a good piece of work, closely stitched in an elaborate pattern, and was said to be typical. She is reputed to have been able to sew as well with her left hand as with her right. "Morning and night she was at them," but, working with her apprentice, she would hardly make two quilts in a week and she never had more than four and six or five shillings for the making.

It was the general rule that customers brought their own materials to be quilted and paid for the work. One quilt a fort-night was said by several people to be the usual rate of output for a professional quilter working alone, but there were many variations. As in the north some worked late "with a candle on the quilt" and others only by daylight. Mrs. Katherine Evans, fifty years ago, worked only eight days on a handsome quilt with a good deal of close stitching in it, which she was still (in 1950) keeping unused for her niece. Mrs. Eleanor Williams said it took her two weeks to make a quilt, working from eight or nine in the morning till about six and only stopping to eat (but her working time must have been shorter in winter, for she only worked by daylight); what I have seen of her work is much rougher than Mrs. Evans's, with simple patterns. Mrs. Colman, an elderly woman quilting for her living, completes a quilt in four or five days and it is well drawn and sewn, though the patterns are big and widely spaced, with no close work. A North Country woman, Mrs. Reaveley, said that in her young days she could make a quilt in two weeks, sitting close at it and working all day and by lamplight too. In all these cases the time included designing and marking the patterns as the work proceeded, but another North Country woman, Mrs. Johnson

9   Quilt by Miss Fmiah Jones, Carmarthenshire

10   Yellow silk quilt, eighteenth century

11   Patchwork quilt with plain white underside, made by Joseph Hedley, known as Joe the Quilter, of Warden, Northumberland, late eighteenth or early nineteenth century.   Owned by Mrs Gibson, Hexham

of Allendale, told how it took herself, her mother and a friend ten days to sew a quilt on which the pattern had already been drawn. This was very close and elaborate work.

Even considering the lower cost of living some fifty years or more ago, and the simple way of life in the villages, one wonders how the labour of the professional quilters really provided them with a *living*; live they did, however, many of them to a ripe old age.

In the North there were also many women who made quilts to order for a living, generally in the rural districts such as Weardale and Allendale and the more northern and westerly parts of Northumberland; in the pit villages quilt clubs (see below) were the rule, though work on club quilts might be interrupted for a "ready-money order." Some workers supplied shops in the towns (as also happened in South Wales), and Miss Humble, already mentioned, had many orders from the U.S.A. through a relative who had emigrated; other orders from America and also Australia and elsewhere far afield have been mentioned.

Quilting was sometimes a sideline to dressmaking—and probably had been so since the eighteenth century or earlier. Miss Annie Williams went at the age of eighteen to learn dressmaking from an old woman in a Carmarthenshire village and "picked up" the quilting at the same time. In the same way Mrs. Parker (Durham) learned to quilt when she served her time with a tailor–dressmaker; afterwards she used to mark the patterns on quilts for her mother and in later years she was well known as a very fine quilter. "Joe the quilter," who is Northumberland's rival to Mari Panteg and who was born about 1750, was intended by his father to be a tailor, and was probably apprenticed to one such and learnt quilting as a part of the trade. By the time Joe began to work on his own, quilted waistcoats and underskirts would be going out of fashion and we can imagine that his taste for gay and elaborate design, indicated by one of his surviving quilts (11), inclined him to concentrate on quilting and patchwork in preference to the more austere kind of tailoring which was becoming the vogue. Certainly he earned his living by those crafts in his old age, until he was murdered, at the age of seventy-six, in 1825, in his cottage near Warden village for the sake of his rumoured wealth (see Appendix II). His work was well known locally and some of it is said to have gone to America.

There are still a number of women in both the quilting areas who supplement small incomes by making quilts for private customers or shops, but the days are past when girls worked as a Durham woman has described: "From leaving school at four-teen until I married I had to sit and quilt, day in and out, and no sooner one out of the frame until another in, and me all the time longing to be out with the other young people; my mother trying to talk to me and me not answering." That memory (of about 1927) gives the darker side of the picture of quilting in the twentieth century.

The village quilter who was a single woman often took an apprentice. In this way Mrs. Lewis learnt to quilt, at the age of sixteen, from Mari Panteg, in order to support her widowed mother who did not come from a quilting family. No payment was made on either side but the pupil did odd jobs for her teacher as well as helping her at the frame. In another case of apprenticeship in Wales the girl lived with her teacher, to whom her parents paid two pounds, presumably for her board for the year. Although Mrs. Thomas (quoted above) spoke of a girl serving her time for two years, one year seems to have been usual in Wales.

In the Weardale and Allendale districts of County Durham and Northumberland there was—and still is—another kind of professional worker in the quilting industry—the pattern-marker, or "stamper" as she is sometimes called. Generally a quilter designs and marks her own patterns (see Chapters Four and Six), but pattern-markers who were not necessarily quilters themselves have been known in the past. In the middle of the eighteenth century a schoolmaster in the village of Mayfield in Sussex, called Walter Gale, who was "undoubtedly a craftsman and a man of parts . . . began to supplement his salary from jobs which varied from decorating inn signs in the neighbour-hood to painting the commandments in the chancel of the church. . . . He drew patterns for ladies' embroidery and helped to create designs for gentlemen's waistcoats. It took him five days of close application to draw the pattern on one quilt, for which he charged nineteen shillings and sixpence. The lady was pleased with the work but (her husband said) it was a pretty deal of money."[1] A London haberdasher in the same century advertised that he drew "all sorts of Patterns" (see Appendix I) which probably included designs for quilting. It seems likely that so long as quilting was in vogue for adorning the clothing and bed furnishings of the fashionable world there would be men skilled in drawing designs for the work, just as there were (even up to about thirty years ago) men "prickers" who designed and pricked the parchments which serve as patterns for pillow-lace makers. The evidence indicates that they studied the technique of the crafts for which they designed and their patterns would therefore be far more suitable than most of the "transfer" designs sold nowadays.

During the latter half of the nineteenth century a certain George Gardiner of Allendale in Northumberland marked patterns on "quilt tops." He had many followers, but I have been unable to discover whether he had any immediate predecessors to link him with the eighteenth-century markers. Like Walter Gale, he was a man of parts; he kept the Allenheads village shop (and a lovely shop it was, as old people in the village will still tell you) in Mill Cottages, Dirt Pot—which is now more politely known as Ropehaugh, though a Youth Hostel preserves the old name. He also trimmed hats, and girls would walk up from Allendale Town or over the fells from Wearhead (some six or seven miles) to get their hats trimmed by his master hand. He introduced a new style of design for quilts, which became very popular in Weardale and throughout Northumberland; he taught his wife's two nieces, who were brought up by the Gardiners, to quilt and mark patterns, and one of them is still active, but his most notable pupil was Elizabeth Sanderson, who served her time with him as apprentice and became even more famous than he as a "stamper." The terms "stamper" and "stamped quilt" were used in the

---

[1] *The Countryman*, "An Eighteenth Century Schoolmaster," by Joan Bellingham. Summer 1952

belief that Miss Sanderson had some method of marking the design by a transfer, but in fact it was drawn, in exact detail, on the material with a blue pencil. She was paid from one shilling and sixpence to two shillings for marking a quilt top, but she could mark two in a day. Whether Walter Gale's five-day design was much larger and more elaborate, or whether he was merely slower because he was inexperienced in quilting, we do not know, but Fig. 14 shows that Miss Sanderson's work was far from simple.

The Misses Johnson in Hexhamshire recalled how Tommy Bell, the packman, had one or two of these drawn quilt tops, as samples, among the goods which he carried from farm to farm, just as pedlars in America sold patterns for quilting, as well as patchwork designs and weaving drafts.[1] The English quilt tops were ordered by farmers' wives who wanted to make something specially grand, or to give to a quilter as a wedding present.

Miss Sanderson was herself a skilled quilter, as her "Red Star" quilt (12) shows, but pattern-marking seems to have been her main livelihood and she left entirely to her sister the management of their farm at Fawside Green, Allenheads. She is said to have "made a tidy bit in her time" and became so well known that she sometimes employed other workers in Allendale to make quilts for her. George Gardiner had died shortly before the turn of the century; Miss Sanderson died in 1934 at the age of seventy-three, but her pupils continue to this day to mark the same type of pattern, which must now have been in use for nearly a hundred years. She taught many girls to quilt and mark patterns; her first apprentice—who is very proud of this priority—was the daughter of a farming butcher at the head of Weardale. On leaving school at the age of fourteen, in the eighteen-nineties, she set out one morning to walk the six miles over the fell to Allenheads, carrying her provisions for the week—bread, butter, sugar and so forth. She served for one year without any payment on either side, going home at the end of each week and setting out again on Monday with her rations. She then became a paid hand, earning about four shillings a

---

[1] *American Quilts and Coverlets*, by Florence Peto.

12 The Red Star quilt, Turkey red and white calico, patched and quilted by Elizabeth Sanderson (1861–1934), Allenheads, Northumberland. Owned by Mrs. William Sanderson The quilted pattern fits into the patchwork shapes The elaboration, in "Gardiner style," of the traditional running feather pattern, is interesting

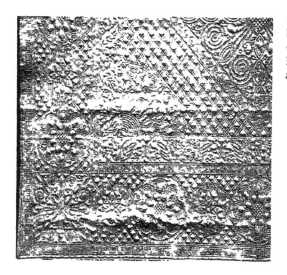

13 Part of a quilt by Miss J M Edwards, Glamorgan. Many traditional units are incorporated in the original design

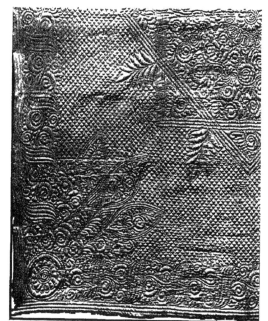

14 Part of a quilt made by Miss E L Hall, Northumberland, about 1900. The pattern, marked by Elizabeth Sanderson, is typical of the style introduced by George Gardiner

week and her board and lodging. As Mrs. Coulthard of Weardale she is still a noted quilter, using the Durham feather patterns as well as the designs she learnt from Miss Sanderson (1), and she has marked many quilt tops for others. Mrs. Peart of Allendale was apprenticed a little later; she also started at the age of fourteen and served for a year without payment, taking her own food. She worked from eight in the morning till seven at night, with an hour off for dinner and half an hour for tea, and she served for six years, being paid two shillings weekly in the second year and finally four shillings. In 1952 she was charging five shillings for marking a quilt top, or seven shillings if the material was silk, and she has had orders from many parts of England and even from Wales, and has had one apprentice herself, who is still at work.

A high-light in Mrs. Coulthard's apprenticeship was the time of Queen Victoria's Jubilee, when they incorporated the Queen's head in a quilt pattern. Mrs. Peart treasures the memory of how she worked on some silk quilts for a local titled lady—an unusual order at that time—and on one occasion helped her teacher draw a quilt top for a Sunderland women's guild to work for Queen Mary.

(2) The ITINERANT QUILTER, who went from farm to farm, staying at each for some weeks to renew the stock of quilts, was a familiar figure of the countryside in South Wales and Radnorshire about fifty years ago. The farmer supplied all the materials and sometimes there was a frame in the farmhouse, but more often the quilter brought her own. Presumably a farmer's wife was too busy herself to make the great number of quilts which would be needed, for the farmhands as well as for the family.

Two sisters at Guisborough in Yorkshire, about 1870–80, used to go to the big houses and farms for several weeks at a time, dressmaking and quilting, being paid a few shillings weekly. In County Durham Mrs. Lough recalled that her great aunt stayed with them for a month each year and quilted for her keep, but this was a family arrangement. I could find no other memory of itinerant quilters in the North, but since dressmaking was often combined with quilting in Wales, it is likely

43

that the North Country dressmaker who periodically went to work in the big houses for a week or so, also made a few quilts. The North Country farmhouse seems to have used just as many quilts as the Welsh one. Was the Welshwoman's time more occupied with farm work, or did she have fewer skilled needlewomen, relatives and hired help, in the house, that she had to depend on the itinerant quilter to maintain the stock of quilts which her North Country counterpart seems to have produced unaided, together with innumerable rag rugs?

"If I rightly remember, she did not have a home; it was going about like that she was," I was told of one Welsh itinerant quilter. "They called her *Y Gwiltreg*; in Llangendeirne and Crwbin district she was." Of another: "The quilting woman would go around the farms making *cwiltiau stafell*" (dowry quilts). Not all of them spent their whole time on the road, some were village quilters working in their own homes and visiting the farms occasionally.

Fifty years ago one of these itinerant quilters was paid ninepence a day, and another at about the same date had from sixpence to a shilling, and another "one shilling daily and food, and a rest day on Sunday." Miss Annie Williams used to go about to farms, staying usually a week or so, till a quilt was finished; at first—this must have been in the 1890's—she was paid tenpence a day. "I started work at eight in the morning and no one'd tell me when to stop. I had my lodging and food; they didn't think anything on the food then." In later years she got as much as three shillings a day, and the same amount was mentioned by another quilter; this is the highest rate heard of. Mrs. Kate Davies (Cardiganshire) writes that "quilters working at farmhouses were paid the same rate as dressmakers, from one and three to one and six a day with board," and Mrs. M. J. Davies of Pembrokeshire knew several quilters who travelled the farms and were paid two shillings and sixpence a day for "making the facings (presumably patchwork) and quilting them." These refer to uncertain dates, probably in the first decade of this century. The custom of travelling the farms seems to have died out many years ago; I have spoken to a number of old quilters who did it in their youth, perhaps until they were

44

married, but I have not heard of it being done in the last twenty years or so.

Sometimes two or three quilters went together; Mrs. Evans of Llanrhystyd (Cardiganshire), when she was apprenticed, used to go with her teacher to work on farms; they made a quilt in from five to seven days. Groups of two or three girls travelling the farms and working together on the frame have been heard of. Several quilters have told us how they took the opportunity to learn the craft from one of these itinerant quilters during her visit to their home. When a farmer's daughter was to be married the quilter would be sent for in good time and might stay a month or more, until six quilts were completed for the dowry.

One gets the impression, in talking to the old ladies who were itinerant quilters in their younger days, that their life was a pleasant and interesting one. Farm fare was good and ample, although they might sleep rough, and for a few weeks they became one of the busy farm community and no doubt shared in the excitement of the wedding preparations when they were making an important part of the dowry.

(3) It seems likely that QUILT CLUBS originated in the Welsh mining valleys and the pit villages of County Durham and Northumberland in the latter part of the nineteenth century. It happened only too often that a miner's wife found herself a widow, or with a disabled husband, and had to seek some means of supporting herself and her children. If she was skilled in the craft of quilting, she thought of her frame; there were her potential customers, hundreds of them, living close together all around her; she could make something gay and pretty for which there was always a need in every household But how was she to find enough money to buy the fifteen yards of sateen, half a dozen reels of cotton and several pounds of wadding needed? Miners were earning low wages and no customer would advance that money; even when she had made her quilt it might be long before any of her neighbours would find ready cash to pay for it. So she thought of the instalment system and started her quilt club.

Mrs. Hope said that her mother in 1887 was left a widow

with five children and "brought them up by quilting", when the four daughters were old enough they helped her at the frame; four working together could turn out four quilts weekly. Once by a terrific effort they made a quilt in a day for a customer about to sail for America. Later they ran their own clubs and all became well known locally as excellent quilters. A Northumberland woman said her mother, working with a neighbour, took "a month or less" to produce a club quilt; Mrs. Hicks and her mother completed one in a fortnight, but Mrs. Frizzel alone turned them out at the same rate.

Mrs. J. Hitchcock, whose mother, a widow with six children, started her quilt club about 1890, recalled that wages were paid fortnightly and so the club contributions were similarly collected, but weekly collection seems to have been more usual. Two shillings was the weekly instalment in a Tweedmouth club between the wars, but one shilling was more often mentioned, or sometimes "one or two shillings a week." Mrs. Graham started her club when her widowed mother-in-law came to live with her; there were several children and only small wages coming in; they made a total of two hundred quilts. The clubs became very popular; one quilter enrolled forty members, another boasted: "Ma mither had the roon of the place for quilts." These instances are from Northumberland, where there were clubs in Amble, Bedlington and Tweedmouth, and County Durham, where information was collected about some dozen clubs in the pit villages and at least two in Jarrow, one run by two maiden ladies in reduced circumstances, and the other by a woman with a ne'er-do-well husband and several children to bring up. There must have been many more in the period from 1887 until textile rationing put an end to them during the 1939–45 war. In the South Wales coalfield in 1928 there were still a number of quilt clubs, but because of the terrible industrial depression at that time they were less flourishing than they had been when most households had one or two men at work.

The Chapel quilt clubs were a great feature of the North, organized like a private club, but for the benefit of chapel funds; they often produced rag mats as well as quilts. The quilt

46

frame, in fact, seems to have taken the place now held by the whist drive as a money-raiser. Amble's (Northumberland) war memorial (1918) was provided by a tremendous communal quilt-making effort by every denomination; about a hundred quilts were finally displayed in the village hall and the fact that there were customers for so many shows the popularity of the work at that time. Several North Country Women's Institutes raised funds for themselves in their early days by raffling quilts which were worked on by members co-operatively. This idea became so popular at one time that a group of Hexhamshire members decided to make one, even though none of them felt equal to designing it. They got a pattern drawn on paper from a Durham woman (the only instance of such a procedure that I have heard of) and cut their own templates. It was set up in a member's house and the middle section was worked first, which seems to have been considered very unusual in Northumberland though it was sometimes done in Wales. Seven or eight members worked on it, but not all at one time; anyone who could spare an hour or two would come in and do a bit. It was a handsome piece of work and well done, but they did not make another. The Northumberland federation recently had a co-operative quilt worked in their Newcastle office by members from all over the county, and this was raffled and brought in a large sum. Mrs. Grays Brown recalled how in her mother's home in the west of Northumberland a frame was set up in the kitchen to raise money for the church in the early years of this century; anyone from the village who could quilt came in and worked on it, the lady of the house supervising the pattern.

It is difficult to give with accuracy the rates of payment in force at various dates because, although many people remember clearly the sums their mother or grandmother earned, they cannot so definitely assign dates. There seems to have been a good deal of variation in payment from one district to another; a quilter's skill and local reputation might enable her to ask a higher fee, but this does not seem to have been always the case. Possibly a local scarcity of village quilters, or some wave of prosperity among their customers, raised the rate of payment. The only written evidence I have come across is a notebook

47

kept by Mrs. Lace of Aberdare when she began to make quilts for orders during a long coal strike in 1907, to help feed her three small children. She was paid five shillings for the first order and from five to twelve shillings for others, according to pattern; during the year she earned ten guineas by making twenty-six quilts—an average of about eight shillings. This tallies pretty well with other people's statements about earnings.

The information on rates of payment at various dates is tabulated in Appendix I, in which an estimate of average weekly earnings is given. Village quilters working for a living may have spent long days at the frame, especially in summer, but those who had quilt clubs were generally the mothers of families and their work must have been interrupted by necessary cooking and housework. The quilter's earnings seem to have been, on the whole, lower in Wales than in the North Country. For instance, Mrs. E. A. Williams (Carmarthenshire) said that her grannie thought herself well paid (probably about 1900) with five shillings, and this was the rate mentioned by several others; but the only worker I heard of earning so little in the North was one in West Auckland whom Mrs. Elizabeth Black used to watch as a girl, who made a club quilt weekly for five shillings, and very rough the work was, with only the simplest patterns, such as *diamonds* with *twist* border.

Quilters are still working for very low wages, which are no longer due to the poverty of the customers (as was the case in the mining districts in the 'twenties); comparatively expensive materials, costing several times the amount paid to the worker, are often chosen. These low rates are earned by workers who are not merely skilled needlewomen; they are also skilled designers and every quilt must be separately planned and marked. To earn a living by quilting has always meant long hours of close application to the frame and yet the old quilters who have lived by their craft do not often speak of it as drudgery; they were always able to enjoy the creative element in the work, to delight in a new pattern, to recall the triumph of achieving a particularly fine one, and that is what they chiefly remember.

48

The Work of the Rural Industries Bureau in Reviving and Developing the Quilting Industry

D URING the first thirty years of this century home quilters and village quilters in the country districts, and club quilters in the mining communities, were at work in South Wales and all over the north of England. By about 1930 the itinerant quilter seldom came trudging with her frame up the rough roads to the Welsh farms, but the farmer could buy quilts in the local shops, for which many village quilters worked. It is impossible to guess the number of these workers but they could certainly have been counted in hundreds, for at the end of 1929 the Rural Industries Bureau had a register of about one hundred and seventy quilters in County Durham and South Wales (chiefly the mining valleys of Glamorgan) who wanted orders for work.

Some efforts had already been made to revive the industry or at least arrest its decay. In Wales Lady Lisburne had encouraged fine work by getting orders for a few quilters, and the Welsh Industries Association had tried to arouse public interest, but the result of these efforts were not very extensive or lasting. In County Durham Miss Alice Armes had stimulated interest in quilting as a home craft amongst the Women's Institutes and the interest spread to the neighbouring county of Northumberland. Miss Armes, herself a fine needlewoman, did good service to the craft of quilting by demanding a high standard of technique and design. Traditional quilting was included in the schedules for Women's Institute handicraft exhibitions, both in these counties and in the National Federation (for which Miss Armes was Handicrafts Organizer); "Durham quilting" began to be widely known amongst people interested in handicraft.

In 1928 I carried out an investigation for the Rural Industries Bureau with the object of discovering some home industry among the women of the stricken mining communities which could be developed for a market beyond those areas. The traditional quilting was the obvious answer to this problem in County Durham; it was known that a few quilters still worked in South Wales but we did not know if any could be found in the mining valleys. Various persons in Monmouthshire and Glamorgan concerned with social, educational or municipal work, when interviewed, declared that quilting was a dead or dying industry in Wales, that no work of any value would be found and that, if it were, no one beyond the Principality would want to buy it. A quilt hung out to dry on a clothes line in a back-yard was my first discovery, which led me, by persistent enquiry, to some dozen quilters. The work they were doing, chiefly for local customers in quilt clubs, was rough, on harsh-coloured sateens and gaudy prints; the designs were very simple, but they were different in style from the Durham patterns and showed possibility of development. Moreover, the quilters declared earnestly that if they had better materials and a rate of payment which would enable them to spend more time on a quilt, they could produce something very much better.

In fact these craftswomen who had fallen on evil days had done good work in their time and knew that they could do it again; their confidence was so impressive that they were given the chance they asked for. The Bureau was persuaded to risk, somewhat reluctantly, the sum of thirty pounds on materials and wages, and orders were sent to the most promising Welsh quilters. It was not difficult to get a few good quilts from Durham as the county federation of Women's Institutes was in touch with good quilters in the pit villages, of whom we chose the neediest. The first exhibition on commercial lines of Welsh and Durham quilting, held in London at The Little Gallery by Miss Muriel Rose in the autumn of 1928, was a great success

50

15 White calico and Turkey red patchwork quilt made by Mrs. Annie
Paulin, Northumberland, about 1900 The quilted twist border and stars
fit into the patches, but the lines of the wine-glass pattern run across the
small red squares

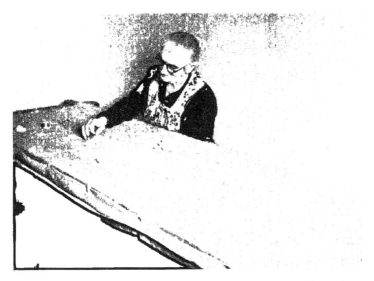

16 Mrs. Amy Thomas, a Welsh quilter, nearing the centre of a big quilt

17 Mrs Lace and Mrs. Olivia Evans demonstrating at the
Welsh Folk Museum, St. Fagan's Castle

and brought in orders to keep the few quilters busy for months. The work shown was crude by present-day standards and had many technical faults, but the Welsh quilters had justified our confidence and sent quilts far better than the club work I had seen in Wales, with more elaborately developed designs of considerable variety.

Other quilters heard of the scheme and asked for orders. It soon became evident that, although there was a fine tradition of quilting still alive in South Wales, with its characteristic patterns quite different from those of the north of England, there were not in the mining valleys enough quilters capable, without some further training, of the very high standard of work which would be needed for the London market. It was therefore decided to organize some classes for the further training of experienced quilters and also to teach new workers. The mining valleys were the Bureau's chief concern and here the standard of work was lowest, so six centres were opened, at Porth in the Rhondda, at Aberdare, Blaina, Merthyr Tydfil, Abertridwr and Splott (Cardiff). In each case a Welshwoman who had learnt quilting in the traditional way, and who knew the Welsh patterns and could do the finest work, was appointed as teacher, and the importance of maintaining the native tradition was always insisted on. Local committees supervised the classes, under the direction of the Bureau.

The classes were financed first by a grant from the Lord Mayor's Coalfields Distress Fund; the Aberdare class was subsidized by a grant from *The Spectator*, which had raised a distress fund of its own, and later the Pilgrim Trust made a grant to the Bureau in aid of the scheme, which was used chiefly to finance trial orders sent to new workers, or to provide quilts which could be used as samples. These grants of money for which no financial return was required, although they amounted in all to not more than eight hundred pounds, were invaluable in establishing the quilting scheme on a sound footing. They made it possible to train and organize a body of women capable of the best craftsmanship, and to have specimens of their work to show.

Amongst many who helped with the organization and running

of these classes, Mrs. Rees, of Porth, Miss Athay of Blaina and Mrs. Phillips of Abertridwr must be specially mentioned for their enthusiastic and devoted service to Welsh quilting, particularly the first named, to whose untiring enthusiasm much of the success of the Porth class was due. Of the teachers, Miss Jessie Edwards at Porth and Mrs. Amy Thomas at Aberdare were outstanding, and their excellent workmanship raised the standard of Welsh quilting to a high level. They are still doing valuable work as teachers of quilting for the local education authorities, as are others who worked in the Bureau's classes, amongst whom Mrs. Edgell is notable for the way in which she has kept a group of quilters working co-operatively at Blaina. At the London end of the scheme Miss Rose, insisting always on good needlework and good design, studying the technique of quilting, giving constructive criticism and taking a personal interest in every worker, constantly inspired the quilters to do better and better work. Many others who cannot be mentioned by name contributed to the success of the scheme.

Pupils in the six classes included women of all ages who had learnt quilting in their youth but could not do fine enough work or were not very skilful in their use of the traditional patterns, and also young girls who learnt for the first time. In several classes, when the course of instruction was finished, the workers continued to meet together as a co-operative group, two or three or even four working at one frame, which was useful for completing large orders quickly. The Porth class was particularly successful in training girls so that they could work together without any difference in the sewing being perceptible.

Quilted work was necessarily costly, but lovers of fine handwork were quick to appreciate it and the versatility of the workers was a great asset. The best of them soon learnt to adapt the traditional patterns to new uses; they made cot quilts, cushions and dressing jackets, as well as bed quilts in all sizes. Quilted garments and cot (or cradle) quilts were not, of course, a really new departure; they had been made in the seventeenth and eighteenth centuries, but these uses of quilting became less general during the nineteenth century and so the designing of patterns for these things had to be learnt anew. Most of the work was done to individual orders, and therein lay much of its attraction.

Two other London retailers were authorized to sell quilts under the Bureau scheme and were supplied with the names and addresses of workers in the north of England and in South Wales. The Bureau continued to supervise the scheme and I visited all the quilters about once a year to discuss problems and new types of work and to ensure that the agreed rates of payment were maintained. The Bureau had established a new type of professional quilter, one who worked for a luxury market beyond her own locality. The hundred and seventy quilters registered in the early days of the scheme did not all become regular workers; the work of some was not good enough, some were too slow or proved unreliable, and, since there was not work enough for all, those who through long unemployment in their families had greatest need of the money were given preference; finally some sixty or seventy quilters were registered as workers.

It was difficult to decide in the beginning what to pay for quilting. It has been shown in Chapter Two how low were the current local rates and obviously more must be paid for fine work. The Trade Board rate for needlework done by outworkers was considered; quilters were consulted and several of them were asked to time themselves accurately on quilts of various sizes. Working on all these data, a minimum rate of one and six-pence per square foot was agreed upon; that is to say, for the work on a quilt of the standard size in South Wales—two and a half by two and a quarter yards—the quilter now received about three pounds sixteen, whereas she had usually been paid by local customers something less than a pound. The workers so quickly responded to the stimulus of better payment and of appreciation that the standard rate of payment under the Bureau scheme soon rose to two shillings per square foot, and two and six was paid for specially fine work or for more troublesome pieces of work, such as cushions and garments. It has since been learnt that in the U.S.A. there is a system of charging for quilting according to the number of reels of cotton used, which is of course a sure indication of the amount of stitching put into a quilt.

The higher rates of payment for quilting under the Bureau scheme do not seem to have had a very far-reaching effect. For local orders quilters today are still making large quilts for as little as twenty-five shillings; inevitably the work done for such orders is of a kind that can be done quickly—large patterns with big unquilted spaces and no close stitching. There are still many workers, however, capable of the best and finest work when they can afford to do it.

It is not easy now, since the end of the Bureau's scheme, to get a quilt made to order. A few good traditional workers, well known in their own localities, are kept busy with orders and often cannot promise a piece of work sooner than six months or even a year ahead. Others cannot spare the time, or have not the inclination, to work regularly for pay. In South Wales there are several young women who can do excellent work at the quilt frame but prefer factory jobs to the meagre livelihood they could earn in that way. The reluctance of customers to recognize that the quilter deserves to be rewarded at a very much higher rate than, for instance, the charwoman has some bearing on the reluctance of the younger quilters to work for pay. Those who do it are the older women who like to continue their settled way of life.

From the start of the scheme in the summer of 1928 until the end of 1929 about £2,287 was paid in wages to the two areas (South Wales and the north of England), being fairly equally divided between them. By the end of three years a total of £10,000 had been paid to the quilters, and thereafter, until the outbreak of war in 1939, about £1,750 was paid on an average each year. The scheme also had more permanent results. The standard of quilting was raised; not only was the neatness and evenness of the sewing improved but great facility was developed in the use of the traditional patterns on quilts of all sizes and other pieces of work. Workers became keenly interested in design and the Welshwomen would search out old patterns and, above all, devise new ones; whereas many of them had formerly been content to repeat with only slight variations a few simple patterns, they were now continually producing fresh ideas. The ancient tradition showed itself to be full of new life.

In County Durham less originality was shown; already some patterns had become standardized there and, as we have seen, some quilters did not even design their own quilts; but some beautiful patterns were produced and new care was taken with details of drawing, such as the shape of the "diamonds" and the way in which a border pattern was contrived to turn the corner.

The scheme aroused throughout South Wales that lively interest in quilting which had already been stimulated in County Durham and Northumberland through the Women's Institutes there. It had come to be regarded as old-fashioned work which was no longer of much interest; it was now realized with some surprise that these elderly women of the villages and mining valleys who sat at their frames in their cottage rooms possessed, and could hand on, the skill and knowledge accumulated by generations of quilters before them, a precious heritage of Welsh traditional culture. Interest spread and the local education authorities arranged many evening classes in quilting to meet a new demand. This demand is still active and there are many L.E.A. quilting classes in both areas, particularly in Glamorgan and in County Durham, though the standard of work done therein is not always of the highest.

With the outbreak of war the Bureau's scheme came to an end. The demand for luxury goods ceased and soon the rationing of textiles raised a new difficulty; moreover, there was other work, and plenty of it, to be done in pit villages and mining valleys and no longer the same desperate need for the earnings which the quilt frame might bring.

CHAPTER FOUR

How Quilts Are Made

SETTING UP

THE quilting frames used in South Wales and in the north of England for the last hundred years at least are of the same pattern and generally do not differ in any important particular from the Devonshire frame made about 1800, of which there is an excellent working drawing in *English Quilting Old and New*. The diagram below shows a frame (or pair of

QUILTING FRAMES - MEDIUM SIZE

SIDE ELEVATION OF STRETCHER
PLAN OF STRETCHER
END VIEW
SIDE ELEVATION OF RAIL
END VIEW
5' 7
PLAN OF RAIL

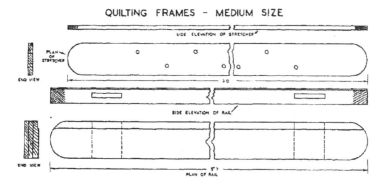

frames, as it is called in the North) of smaller size made recently in Weardale. Probably the design of this simple apparatus was standardized long ago.

It consists of two long bars, the runners (of oak in many of the older frames), rounded or straight-sided ("sheer" as a Durham woman described them), and two cross-pieces, the stretchers, which fit through slots in the bars and are kept in place by wooden or metal pegs fitted into holes. In the rectangle thus formed—the width of which can be varied by a choice of holes for the pegs—the quilting materials are held securely. A strip of webbing is tacked along one edge of each runner so that the material for the underside of the quilt may be sewn to it. The frame in use must be rested at its ends on two supports to hold it steadily at a convenient height for working; commonly it is laid across two straight chair backs, but a quilter regularly at work may have trestles made for her frame. Marie Webster describes the quilting frame generally used in America, which is similar to the Welsh or English one, and mentions a "more pretentious" kind with its own supporting framework, which is shown in a photograph. A frame "with its own legs," which was heard of in Wales, was probably similar to this.

A frame made in Weardale some fifty years ago and now owned by Mrs. Graham Peart (8) has a wooden ratchet at one end of each runner, so that the quilt may be wound on to the runner as it is worked, instead of being taken out and set up again (see below). The opposite end of each runner finishes in a wooden peg which fits through a hole in the stretcher; a large nail dropped through a hole bored transversely through the peg near its end keeps the stretcher in place. The photograph shown in the American book referred to above shows a similar device. Another Weardale quilter had an old frame in which the runners could be moved along the stretchers, and fixed, by a screw, instead of the usual hole-and-peg arrangement. Both the ratchets and the screw seem to be useful devices and it is surprising that they are not more often found. In America it seems customary to hold the stretchers and runners together at the corners by means of screw clamps, according to Ruth Finley and Florence Peto. The former also mentions that "every household had a set of at least four quilting chairs" with straight backs.

The method of "setting up" a quilt in the frame is shown in the series of pictures of a Weardale quilter at work (22-27); pattern-marking, shown in Figs. 18-21 of this series, is dealt with later in the chapter. Each side of the material for the underside (the bottom cover or backing) of the quilt is sewn to the webbing on a runner (22); the stuff is then wound round one runner until only a convenient width for working (about eighteen inches or two feet) is left exposed, the stretchers are put through the runners and the pegs put in so as to give the correct tension (23). The material must not be stretched taut, but fixed so as to give a certain amount of play and make it easy to sew with a running stitch through three thicknesses. Some writers recommend a round embroidery frame for small pieces of work, but since such a frame is designed to hold the material taut it is difficult to adjust it for quilting.

It is generally considered best to set up the whole *length* of a quilt in the frame and roll up some of the width, so that the work is started along one side. As it proceeds the stretchers are, from time to time, taken out, the quilted part is rolled round a runner and a fresh piece exposed. In the picture of Mrs. Amy Thomas at work (16), the first side of a large quilt has been completed and rolled and she is reaching the centre. If the quilt were set up widthways in the frame and work started across one end, the seams (generally two) make ridges and thus tend to pull the covers unevenly across the part that is being quilted. Nevertheless most quilters, if they have to make a quilt too long to go lengthways in the frame, will set it up widthways, though one Welsh quilter told me that she was so averse to doing this that when she had an order for some quilts nine feet long for a Carmarthen hotel she had a frame specially made to take this unusual length. A small piece of work may be set up in its whole extent in the frame and not have to be moved until the quilting is finished; this is the case with the cot quilt on which Mrs. Lace is working in the foreground of Fig. 17.

To return to our quilt, which we have left with only the bottom cover set up in the frame; the padding is now laid on carefully so that it is of even thickness all over (24). If it is cotton-wool or wadding (see Chapter Five) it should first be warmed to fluff it and so that the needle will go through nicely. The material for the upper side of the quilt (the top cover) is now laid on and held firmly on the quilter's near side of the frame by a tacking thread through all three thicknesses (25); it is then smoothed over the padding and fastened down on the far side of the frame by tacking threads, pins or needles. These last are preferred by some quilters to pins, which would make bigger holes in the material. The spare width may be loosely rolled and pinned up to keep it off the floor (26). The work is thus held in place between the runners; to hold it in the other direction, between the stretchers, a length of tape is pinned (or preferably needled) to all three layers at each end and passed round the stretcher at three-inch intervals (27). The work is now ready for sewing. The pattern may have been marked before the work was set up, or it may be done at this stage; the methods of marking are described below (see p.43 et seq.).

SEWING

Traditional wadded quilting is sewn with a running stitch. The quilter holds her left hand under the work and, as one craftswoman described it, she senses where the needle will come through and helps it back. Her right thumb is extended at every stitch to press the material down slightly just ahead of where the needle will come up (28, 30, 32, 33). As another good Durham quilter said: "There's an art in the stitch—not lifting the material and not digging down into it." Another North Country woman, the owner of some fine old quilts, when asked if she was herself a quilter, said no; she had tried it but "I can get the needle doon but I canna get it back oop!"

It will be obvious that a quilter cannot turn her work, as an embroideress or plain sewer does, to enable her to sew always in the most convenient direction. She sits all the time on the same side of the frame and when sewing a curved line she must be able to adjust her hold on the needle so that it runs comfortably round the curve, using her thumb nail, instead of the ball of her thumb, to help the needle up (29, 31).

A number of stitches are taken up on the needle at once, before it is pulled through. There is no point in making the stitches very small, so long as they are even; very tiny stitches may give the line a spotty effect. A skilled quilter works quickly and with a rhythm which produces true, straight lines or flowing curves. This rhythm is perhaps the most important feature of the technique.

Several needles may be in action at once. For instance, in stitching the *twist* pattern (p.81), or the *basket* background on which the quilter is at work in Figs. 28-31, with a number of parallel lines, it may be best to have a separate needle in each line and carry each one a little way forward in turn.

It is not true that you "must prick your finger with every stitch," though a beginner may do this and leave little marks of her wounds on the work. In fact it is the thumb of the right hand which is more likely to get sore from being pricked, but one excellent worker told me that she avoids this by dipping her fingers in surgical spirit before and after working.

A knot is made in the end of the cotton when starting a fresh needleful, but it must be pulled sharply through so that it remains unseen in the padding. The last stitch of a needleful must be made secure and the end of cotton brought out through the material and cut off short. Sewing cotton No. 40 is generally recommended for quilting any material and is made in many shades; it should be chosen to match the top cover. Some quilters like to use sewing silk on silk materials. Mercerized cotton (such as *Sylko*) is unsuitable.

What will be the upper side of the quilt, or the outside of a garment, must always be on top in the frame; every stitch must of course go right through the three layers and both the stitches and the spaces between them should look the same on both sides. An experienced quilter may claim that she can always tell which was the uppermost side in the frame, but no unevenness in the stitching should show this; probably the method of setting up and working makes the underside a little flatter.

When any kind of "patched" work, particularly applied work, is used for the top cover of a quilt (see below, p.16, *et seq.*) there may be some difficulty in carrying the running stitch through the extra thicknesses made by the turned-under edges of the "patches." The North Country custom of quilting patchwork in accordance with the pieced pattern avoids this difficulty only when it is strictly carried out (12, 15, 34). The Welsh worker's designs, on the other hand, generally show a fine disregard of the patches (35) and possibly one or two stab stitches may sometimes have been necessary in crossing the difficult area.

Backstitching can be seen on some eighteenth-century quilts; there was a fashion for it in yellow silk on linen, perhaps because an unbroken line of contrasting colour defined more clearly a complicated pattern which the rather dull surface of linen would not throw up vividly in relief. But the untidiness of the reverse side of backstitching is a disadvantage in work in which "reversibility" should be a characteristic feature. It may be used effectively on a cushion cover, of which only one side will be on show.

When several quilters work together they usually sit along one side of the frame, with perhaps one at each end. As many as six can certainly work in this way, four at a side and two at the ends. It is important to keep the work smooth and the padding spread evenly; if the quilt is worked from both sides of the frame there is a danger that it may be cockled in the middle of the strip worked on. Therefore many good quilters will say that they never allow workers to sit on both sides of the frame and some even run a tacking thread zigzag over the quilt when several are working together, to make sure the three layers are kept in place. In the communal village quilting of the old days, and in quilt clubs in which a group of women worked together to turn out quilts as quickly as possible, the sewing was sometimes done from both sides at once. A wider strip of work can, of course, be set up in the frame when this is done, and so time is saved by fewer "rollings."

Ruth Finley describes a method of working unheard of in this country, with a frame of which all four pieces, stretchers and runners, are the same length—ten to twelve feet—and in which the whole quilt is first set up. Workers sit round all four sides of this vast area and "all reachable space on each of the four sides is quilted." Then the ends are rolled, another piece worked, rolled again, and so on. She mentions "five or six rollings" to complete a quilt. This frame was probably invented to suit the American "quilting bee" when, a patchwork cover having been finished, a large party of neighbours was invited to come over for the day and help make the quilt.

Most quilters stitch one side of the quilt first (or one end, if it is set up widthways), then the middle and lastly the other side or end; but a few start on the middle section, particularly if the design is planned with a centrepiece. Others have been known to work both sides (or ends) before they start on the middle section.

VARIOUS FRAMES

It will be clear that the runners of the frame must be rather longer than the full length (or width) of the largest quilt likely to be made. The old frames were usually between eight and nine feet long, since the standard size for bed quilts was two and a half yards by two and a quarter. A quilter can seldom tell you the exact length of her frame; she will say that it will take a quilt of such and such a length. There is said to be an ancient frame of unusual length in the village of Llandarrog, which was borrowed locally for making specially big wedding quilts.

The space needed for this eight or nine feet long apparatus is an undeniable drawback to quilting as a home craft, particularly for people in modern houses with small rooms and for those who like the sitting-room to look always elegant. A Northumberland woman living in a smart little bungalow, who had often worked with her mother on big quilts in their former farmhouse home, said she would not undertake one now: "I should have the frame standing in the sitting-room for a month!" But at one time a piece of fine handiwork in the making, even in the best room, would only have been reckoned to the maker's credit, and it would be so today by anyone with a sense of true values. "Quilting was done in the parlour," said one old lady firmly, and many quilters did, and still do, devote their parlours to the quilt frame. It had its place too, and with room to spare, in many an old-fashioned farmhouse kitchen. A group of quilters in Blaina (Monmouthshire) have, since the time of the quilting

18 A County Durham quilter considers her templates

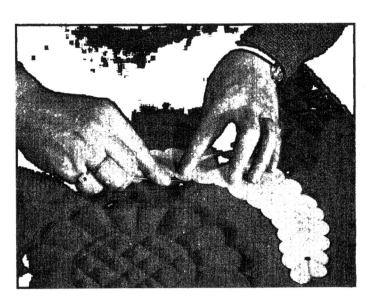

19 She needle-marks the outline of a template on the top cover

20 She uses a penny to mark the middle of the feather pattern

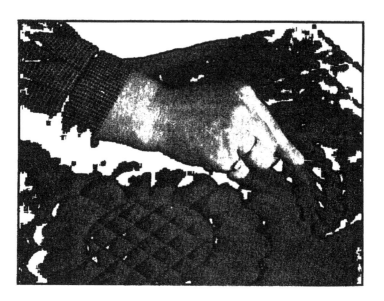

21 She marks the other lines freehand

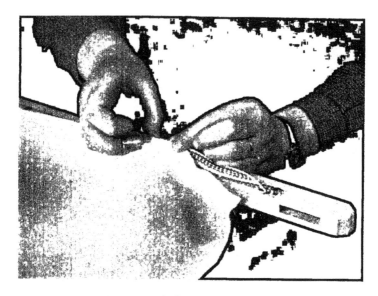

22 Oversewing the bottom cover to the runner

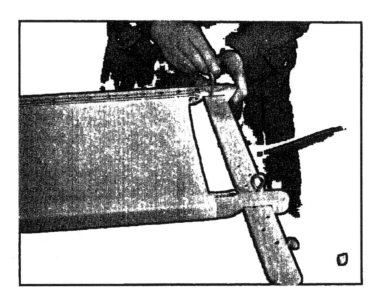

23 The stretcher is fixed with pegs to give the right width

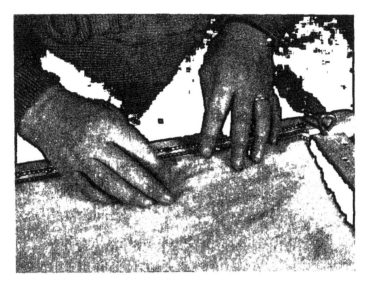

24 Wadding is laid carefully on the bottom cover

25 Tacking thread through all three thicknesses holds work
in place along near side of frame

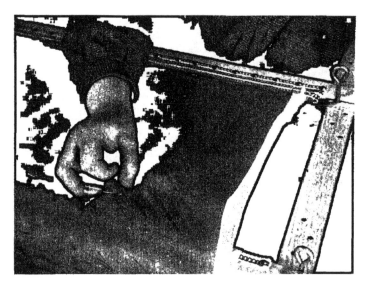

26 The three layers are ' needled'' along the far side of the frame

27 Tape is "needled" to all three thicknesses and looped round
the stretcher at 3-in intervals

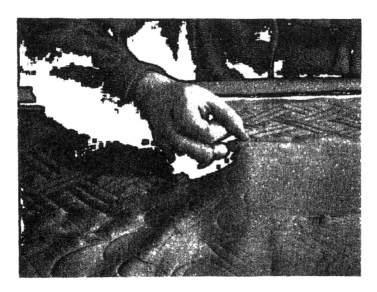

28 Sewing the quilt Note the number of needles, some in use and some spares

29 Working in the opposite direction, the needle is pointed away
from the quilter

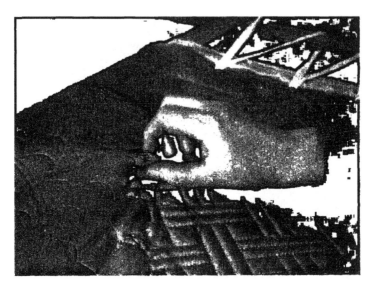

30 Note the number of stitches taken up on the reedle

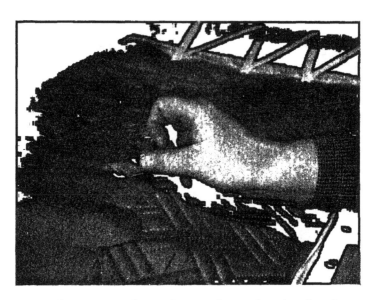

31 The same actions shown in Figs 28 and 29 are shown here from the worker's point of view

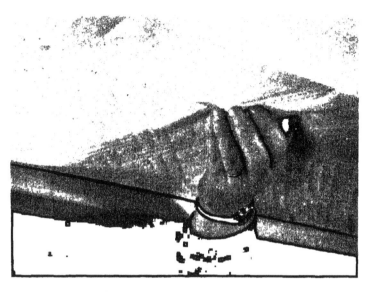

32 The quilter's left hand under the work; she feels the needle coming down and

33 . she helps it up to the surface again

class set up there by the Rural Industries Bureau, continued to rent an attic room large enough for their several frames to stand in.

Once, in County Durham, I was examining a partly worked quilt in its frame, which stood across the middle of the kitchen, reaching from one wall to the other, when there was a knock at the door and a man's voice called: "Can we come in?" The woman hastily swathed her quilt (of delicate pale silk) in an old sheet before calling in her husband and son, who, black from the pit, crawled carefully under the frame and went on into the scullery for their baths. A frame may be upended against the wall when not in use, but the most ingenious solution of this problem of space was to fix two pulleys in the ceiling, by means of which the frame was hauled up, to hang there out of the way until wanted again.

Nowadays many quilters have, as well as their full-sized frames, smaller ones for cot quilts, cushion covers and other small pieces of work. Cradle quilts and pieces of work as small as, for instance, a baby's bonnet were certainly quilted long ago, but no small frame, nor any cradle quilt made before about 1930, was found in Wales in the course of my survey. A Carmarthenshire woman tells me that cradle quilts were made on small frames long before that and, in a Cardiganshire village, cradle quilts were remembered in use some seventy or eighty years ago, but in this case no one was sure whether small frames were used. At least three quilters in County Durham possess small "pairs of frames" of considerable age with runners a yard or a yard and a half long. Probably such frames were in general use in the past, but during the nineteenth century, when large bed-covers and petticoats came to be almost the only things quilted, they presumably went out of use and were destroyed. Quilters in both districts carried out during the nineteen-thirties, under the Rural Industries Bureau's scheme, many orders for cot quilts and cushions and, for the sake of convenience, had small frames made by local carpenters, so now they are common again. The frame shown on p.34 could easily be made in a smaller size.

Some strange tales were told in Wales of small quilts being

set up in picture frames or on the legs of a table turned upside-down! I never traced such a story to its source and if these peculiar procedures were ever really adopted it can only have been the result of misguided ingenuity when a frame was lacking. Quilting without a frame was also mentioned by several people and after many enquiries I did find, in Llangwm (Pembrokeshire), one woman who with her grandmother had made many quilts on the kitchen table with weights (usually flat-irons) "to keep it stiff." Several specimens of this work were seen, the crudest and roughest kind of quilting imaginable, stitched in more or less straight lines running in various directions at random, with no attempt whatever at a pattern. The covers were made of a rough kind of patchwork in large strips and squares. In this village apparently no other kind of quilting was known. An old lady in Cardiganshire remembered her grandmother making cradle quilts on a table with a stone at each corner, but this also must have been a makeshift job, perhaps by someone who was not a regular quilter and had no frame. Certainly the Llangwm quilts bore out the verdict of other quilters who, when asked about the possibility of quilting without a frame, said, "No good quilter would ever do it." I feel sure that no good pattern quilting ever was, or could be, done in this way.

SEAMS AND EDGES

For a large quilt several widths of material must be joined, and if, for instance, thirty-six-inch wide material is used for a quilt nearly six feet in width, one length should be split to avoid a seam down the middle of the quilt. It is necessary to cut off the selvages of certain materials because they would show through. There are two opinions about how the seams should be sewn—by hand or by machine. On the one side it is said that since quilting is essentially handwork no machinework should be allowed; on the other side, a skilled quilter may say that she prefers to join at least the seams of the bottom cover by machine because these are subject to a certain amount of pull and machine stitching is stronger. She may agree that on certain materials hand sewing will give a better appearance, and may therefore use it on the top cover. Doubtless back-stitching by hand *can* be as strong as machine sewing, but it is a tedious job on long seams. Certainly a sewing machine was part of the equipment of quilters in the past, since the time when it became available fairly cheaply, but it may be argued that this is only because they were driven by their low wages to seize any available short cut to quick output. A Northumberland woman told me with fondness and amusement how her father bought her first sewing machine, a "Howe," at a horse fair for half a crown and got it repaired for another half-crown; she was just starting to work professionally as a quilter and needed a machine, and although there were many jokes about it, she used it for years.

There are several ways of finishing the edges of a quilt, which is done after it is taken out of the frame. The method generally recommended is to turn in the edges of top and bottom covers and sew them with one or two straight lines of running stitch. This is a traditional finish, but some old quilts are finished with piping, which makes a nice firm edge but is more troublesome to do. Patchwork quilts were sometimes finished by turning the bottom cover over the top (the patchwork) and hemming or running it down. I have seen old quilts bound all round with a wide strip of material cut on the cross, but I think this was done at a later date to repair a frayed edge. Some modern quilters finish the quilted border about two inches from the edge and turn in the edges of the material with a single line of running stitch, leaving a wide unquilted band all round, but this looks clumsy and is only a work-saving device.

PATTERN-MARKING

I have left the subject of how the pattern is marked until last, although, of course, it must be done at an early stage, because there are so many opinions about when and how it should be done. On every point of technique there is some difference of opinion, but quilters are inclined to be more dogmatic about the patterns and how they should be marked than about any other point in their craft.

There are two main systems: to mark the whole quilt before

some fifty years ago, but there seems no way of finding out what method was used in the time beyond living memory. Ruth Finley says that in America quilt patterns which were bought stamped on paper were traced on to the material with a spur rowel or a rowelled dressmaking wheel and then marked with coloured chalk or pencil. Possibly the old method of "pouncing," with powdered charcoal rubbed through holes pricked along the pattern lines in paper or some stiffened material, may sometimes have been used. But some old quilts are so free and easy in their drawing that they would seem to have been quilted with very little marking of any sort.

The blue-pencil marking was used, presumably by George Gardiner, certainly by Elizabeth Sanderson and all her followers, because lines which would show up clearly and would not rub out were necessary when the marked top was bought to be quilted by someone to whom the pattern was unfamiliar. It is not a good method of marking because the blue lines show, even after the quilting is done, until the quilt is washed. But some old ladies in the North cherish quilts marked by George Gardiner and deliberately keep them unwashed "so that the marks will show"!

The patterns on the marked quilt tops for sale had to be drawn complete in every detail and some quilters marking for themselves put in all the fillings, but others only outline the main shapes (units) of the pattern, by drawing round templates, before setting up the quilt in the frame; the details (fillings) are put in as they work. Some North Country women do not mark the material at all before it goes into the frame; even when the quilt has a centre pattern they find the middle point of the middle width only when they reach that section. This is said by some to be the old method; in any case, the "strippy" quilts (see Chapter Five) were probably always marked as the work went on, because their quilted patterns, all in strips running the length of the quilt, could easily be dealt with in this way.

TEMPLATES

Every North Country quilter to whom I have talked has a collection of templates for marking patterns (see Fig. 18).

They are cut from card or stiff paper or sometimes from plywood or tin. She will have the units which she uses most often in several different sizes. Some of the templates probably came from her mother or grandmother, others she has made herself and some may have been cut by her husband or son. There is some borrowing of templates, but generally a quilter regards them as her copyright, though when she notes an unfamiliar and attractive pattern unit on any quilt she happens to see, she will go home and "bother with brown paper," as one of them put it, until she has cut the template.

The templates give the outline of the shapes in the pattern, and the filling is put in "freehand." Mrs. F. Fletcher remembers that when she first went to live in Weardale, some twenty years ago, she used to watch Mrs. Foster who kept the village shop at Wearhead, and who had been apprenticed to one of Miss Sanderson's pupils, drawing quilt tops on the counter, using a few templates but marking a great deal of the elaborate scroll-work by eye.

In Wales, the usual method of marking a quilt is to measure the material before it is put in the frame and indicate the centre and perhaps a few other features, such as border lines, and sometimes to mark it off into the sections which are to be set up and worked at one time, but to mark the pattern, bit by bit, only when the work is in the frame. Some Welsh quilters use no templates and mark the pattern merely with the help of their usual tackle—tailor's chalk, string, a ruler, needles and thread and pins. Measurements and chalk marks, tacking threads, needle-marks and perhaps a few pins stuck upright, are the only guide they need for sewing quite a complicated pattern.

A Carmarthenshire quilter, describing how her mother used to mark her centre pattern, said "she marked the centre and drew a circle with chalk and drew in the spokes; then she added scallops round the edge." Certainly many good quilters can do a surprising amount of freehand drawing with firm, flowing lines, but the pattern on the quilt I saw which had been worked in this way was noticeably irregular. Miss Eleanor Evans of Carmarthenshire told me that her mother never used chalk;

she cut paper templates when she needed them, but often she marked only with pins and sometimes with tacking threads as well. Fig. 35 shows one of her quilts, which is beautifully regular in drawing. Miss Evans herself, when working the spiral pattern generally known in Wales as a *rose* or *round* but called by her a *snail creep*, indicates its centre, measures from that and makes another mark to show where its outer edge will come. She starts stitching in the centre and works round and round by eye till she reaches the outside mark. A Cardiganshire quilter

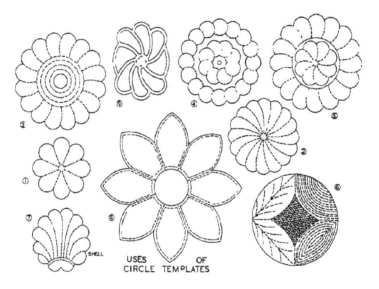

SHELL

USES   OF
CIRCLE   TEMPLATES

uses a template for this pattern, to mark only its outermost line, and works it in the same way. Some others use a template in spiral form, so that the complete pattern is marked. These instances show how much variety in methods of marking there can be and how rash it would be to say that any one method is correct, or even better than others.

Generally the Welshwoman seems less concerned to preserve her templates, and you seldom find in Wales the permanent wooden or tin ones. More often they are cut from paper to suit the quilt in hand. Some quilters mark a circle by attaching the

79

end of a suitable length of thread to the centre and marking the outline either with the threaded needle or with a piece of chalk tied at the end of the thread. A long, straight line may be marked by stretching a chalked string taut above the material and plucking it sharply. In both districts plates or kitchen pans may be brought into use instead of a template to mark a circle. "The fun we were having making designs," said an old Carmarthenshire quilter reminiscently; "many a time we were putting a pan upside down so as to have the circle even."

Every quilter has always at hand, on her dresser or in her kitchen, numerous templates, in the form of cups, glasses,

FILLINGS

WINE GLASS-TWO TEMPLATES   SHELL OR MOTHER OF THOUSANDS   DIAMONDS-TWO TEMPLATES

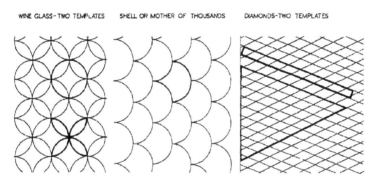

saucers, plates and pans, for marking various sizes of circle—a shape which is probably found on ninety per cent. of Welsh quilts and certainly on very many North Country ones. A coin from her purse may be used for the smallest size. By the filling it may be turned into many different patterns (see Diagram, p. 79) ; the edge may be scalloped and straight spokes added, or else curved, radiating lines; with the lines curving from a point on the circumference, instead of from the centre, it is a *shell* (see centre and border of Fig. 36); developed into a spiral it is a Welsh *rose*; with a different filling again it may be a *plate* or *pincushion*. One Durham woman reversed the scallops and called it *gramophone horn*. There are numerous names for all these patterns (see Chapter Six). One Northumberland woman calls her scalloped circle template a *star*, and names any pattern made from it a *star*, whether it is filled in as a *rose* or as a *shell*.

A feather similar to the one being marked in Fig. 20 was called by Mrs. E. Black a threeha'penny feather because she used a penny and a halfpenny to mark the centre.

Various quilters may use quite different templates to mark the same pattern. For instance, *diamonds*, are usually drawn with an ordinary flat ruler or with a special square-section

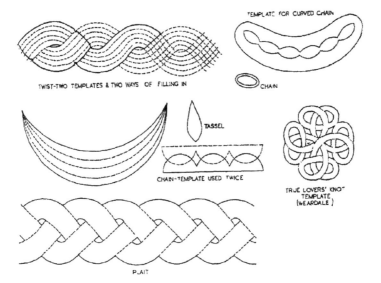

TWIST–TWO TEMPLATES & TWO WAYS OF FILLING IN

TEMPLATE FOR CURVED CHAIN

CHAIN

TASSEL

CHAIN–TEMPLATE USED TWICE

TRUE LOVERS' KNOT TEMPLATE (WEARDALE)

PLAIT

inch-wide one, but some quilters mark them with a large triangular template, starting from a straight border and moving the template along (see p.80). The usual template for marking the *twist* (or *cable*) is lemon-shaped, but Mrs. Mason in County Durham has a different one (see above) and Mrs. Dixon in Northumberland called the pattern *plate* because she marked it with a plate. The beautiful and popular pattern of overlapping circles (clearly shown in the middle of Fig. 37) may be marked with a round template; the *wine-glass* used when it is on a small scale gives it one of its names; but many quilters prefer to use a four-lobed template (see p.80), which perhaps suggested another of its names, *cuddy's lug* (donkey's ear).

There are parts of certain patterns which must always be marked freehand, such as the curlicues on the "stamped" quilts already mentioned (5, 14) and the various *baskets of flowers, sprays of flowers* and *flower pots*, so often used in the West Country, as Mrs. Hake showed,[1] and found, too, on nineteenth-century quilts both in South Wales and in the north of England.

[1] *English Quilting Old and New*, by Elizabeth Hake.

CHAPTER FIVE

The Materials

I. THE PADDING

A QUILT is a textile sandwich; between the top and bottom covers is the padding, which is put in for the sake of warmth and is held in place by the stitching. That is the primary function of the sewing, but its secondary purpose is to form patterns by outlining shapes; in these spaces between the lines of stitching the padding rises up, so that the pattern is in relief. Thus a padding which is springy and stands up well where it is not held down by stitches will give the quilt a better decorative effect.

In Britain, the wool from local flocks must have been the original padding for quilts long before cotton-wool, an imported material, came into use. According to the *Encyclopædia Britannica* cotton-wool was used in England for candle wicks in the thirteenth century but did not, apparently, become well known until much later, since a document of 1621 finds it necessary to describe it as "a sort of bombast or down, being a fruit of the earth, growing upon little shrubs or bushes, brought into this kingdom by the Turkey merchants, from Smyrna, Cyprus, Acra and Sydon, but commonly called cotton-wool." Evidence for its occasional use in quilts at a date much earlier than is generally supposed is to be found in *A Compendyous Regyment or a Dietary of helth*,[1] by Andrew Boorde, 1542, who gives this advice: "Let your nightcap be of scarlet, and this, I do advertise you, to cause to be made a good thick quilt of cotton, or else of pure

[1] Quoted by John Dover Wilson in *Life in Shakespeare's England*. Penguin Books, 1944.

flocks or of clean wool, and let the covering of it be of white fustian, and lay it on the featherbed that you do lie on; and in your bed lie not too hot nor too cold, but in a temperance.''

Although Andrew Boorde was evidently rather a faddist, it is clear that by the middle of the sixteenth century raw cotton was well enough known to be considered as a possible alternative to flocks or wool for padding quilts. The evidence of surviving quilts suggests that wool continued to be the more usual padding, but it is interesting to note Ruth Finley's statement that before the Revolution (that is, up to the third quarter of the eighteenth century) most of the materials for American quilts, *including wadding*, were imported from England. Although cotton was cultivated in Virginia as early as 1621, it was not a staple crop until about 1760; after that the local plantations presumably supplied the padding for American quilts. But Florence Peto describes the earliest surviving American quilts (made about 1750–70) as padded with softest wool, whereas Ruth Finley writes that ''not infrequently quilts were filled with fleece, out of necessity rather than choice'' because the fleece was inadequately washed, retained much oil and ''gave forth a disagreeable odour'' in heat or a damp atmosphere. These conflicting statements suggest that some immigrants had been accustomed in their home country to the use of wool, whilst others had never used it before and did not realize how thoroughly it had to be scoured. Had they, or their mothers, been using cotton-wool already in England, or were they Dutch settlers, amongst whom there are said to have been many quilters?

In this country sheep's wool seems to have continued to be the more usual padding until the nineteenth century; the countrywoman could probably get it more easily and cheaply than the exotic cotton-wool. Any quilt or quilted garment made before about 1800 which I have been able to examine is padded with sheep's wool. With the great expansion of the cotton textile industry in this country after the perfection of spinning machinery towards the end of the eighteenth century, cotton-wool presumably became generally and cheaply available. At first it would be the raw product, full of dust and seeds,

34 Red and white patchwork quilt made by Mary E. Carr at Blyth,
Northumberland, about 1870–75, before her nineteenth birthday; owned
by her daughter, Mrs Grays Brown The patches are squares of two sizes;
the quilted pattern is fitted into these squares and the border

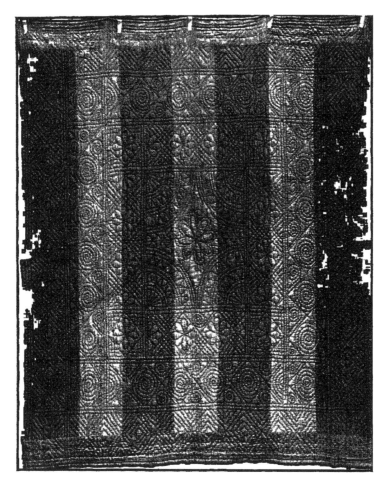

35 Late nineteenth-century quilt of strip patchwork in fawn and red
sateen, made by H Evans. Owned by her daughter, Miss Eleanor Evans,
Carmarthenshire. The quilted design is planned without regard to the
patches. The spiral pattern is known in this family as *snail creep*

which the quilter herself would probably card as she had carded sheep's wool. Between 1820 and 1830 the manufacture began, in the Manchester district, of cotton-wool from cotton of shorter staple than that used for spinning. In the factory it is cleaned and carded, by which process the fibres are all laid one way so that the substance becomes a smooth layer instead of a tangled mass. This would be the cotton-wool bought by the pound which quilters speak of as having been used "in the old days"; some still use it in preference to *wadding*, which has been passed through a size-trough before drying to give it the "skin" or backing.

Cotton-wool is sold in pound packets, each containing a rolled-up sheet which opens out to about forty-eight by forty-five inches; it is bleached or "grey" (actually a pale off-white) and of various thicknesses and qualities. The best quality is beautifully soft and clean and its price at the present time is about the same as that of sheep's wool. With care in handling it can be spread on the bottom cover of the quilt almost as easily as the skin-backed wadding. The latter is also sold as bleached or grey, in various weights and qualities, usually in twelve-yard lengths thirty-six inches wide Many quilters prefer it because the skin makes it easier to handle without disturbing its even thickness. There is also a kind of wadding with a harder sized back for use by clothing manufacturers in shoulder pads and other padding; possibly those quilters who complain that the skin makes wadding difficult to sew through have mistakenly used this kind.

By the latter part of the nineteenth century cotton-wool and wadding had become universally popular for padding quilts. In the North it seems to have ousted wool earlier and more completely; possibly because all the wadding manufacturers were in the Manchester area and their products may have spread more slowly to South Wales. A few people in the North still remember the use of wool. A Westmorland woman said that her grandmother (born in 1810) had told her that sheep's wool was used before cotton-wool, "which was cleaner," came in. Another Westmorland woman knew of its use, more recently, in a small quilt "to go across the foot of the bed" (As a remedy for cold feet?) but never in a large one. I have been told that the old "stobbed quilts" of Weardale sometimes had a padding of wool between their thick covers, but they were not quilted, strictly speaking, being merely held together by threads knotted through them with the ends standing up in tufts. The Misses Johnson of Hexhamshire have an old homespun quilt padded with wool which was probably made very early in the nineteenth century (compare Fig. 3); the early American wool-interlined quilts described by Florence Peto, of linsey-woolsey, the household staple, strictly a home product, home-dyed blue and buff, quilted with loosely spun linen thread, must have been in the same tradition.

The pieces of quilted silk intended for a petticoat (6), of mid-eighteenth-century date, found in Northumberland, are interlined with a thin layer of wool (Cheviot, says the owner, a farmer's wife) dyed to match the blue silk exactly. Some quilted underskirts of the same period in the Victoria and Albert Museum also have their wool padding dyed to match the satin, and one is mysteriously padded with wool of rather deep blue although the covering materials are of an oyster shade. Was too much wool, perhaps, dyed blue for some other quilted work and the surplus used here because the satin was thick enough to avoid any danger of the blue colour showing through? Certainly wool, in its natural tone, does sometimes show through thin silk of a pale colour and gives it a slightly dirty look. Another quilt with wool padding, seen in Westmorland, is believed to have been made in Northumberland in the reign of Queen Anne; this is of parchment-coloured silk backed with linen scrim, in beautiful condition.

Even in the sheep-farming districts of Wales, though sheep's wool did not go entirely out of use, cotton-wool seems to have been more commonly used by quilters during the last century. Of forty-eight Welsh quilters (most of them over fifty) who replied to a questionary, only six mentioned no other padding than wool, though over thirty used it sometimes. Twenty-five used blankets and twenty-two wadding. Most of them used various kinds of padding according to the tastes and resources of customers and to what was thought suitable. For instance, "flannel quilts were usually padded with wool or an old blanket; print quilts were padded with cotton."

Wool is unquestionably a warmer material than cotton, but new cotton-wool or wadding, in its fluffy state, should be effective in holding warm air. It is generally agreed, however, that a wool padding remains springier after washing; cotton tends to felt and flatten so that the quilted pattern is difficult to see after much laundering, and the quilt's capacity for holding warmth must be diminished. Wool is generally a lighter material than cotton, but the amount of wadding used in a quilt does not weigh a great deal more than a similar thickness of wool padding. For instance, a full-sized quilt thinly padded would need nine yards of wadding, weighing about two and a quarter pounds, or from one and three-quarter to two pounds of wool; thickly padded, in the old-fashioned style, it might have as much as twenty-four yards of wadding (six pounds) or four pounds of wool. Lightness of weight was not always considered an advantage, for many quilters of a former generation definitely aimed at "something heavy to put on the bed."

The outstanding advantage of cotton-wool or wadding is that it is bought ready for use. Sheep's wool must first be thoroughly scoured to remove dirt and grease; it can be bought "clean scoured for quilting" from some of the Welsh woollen mills, but even then it may need further washing. It must next be carded, to lay the staple evenly, and then spread, bit by bit, on the material, being carefully scrutinized for dark specks of grease which would make marks on the quilt. A good deal of time must also have been spent in picking the hard seeds out of the early cotton-wool, for they are liable to interrupt the passage of the needle, but even so, this padding must have been less troublesome to deal with than wool, and that probably accounts for its popularity as soon as it was easily available to the ordinary village or farmhouse quilter.

Possibly, too, many quilters found difficulty in getting suitable wool to line their quilts, for it should be soft, not coarse, and lambs' wool is best. Some Welsh wool is suitable, but not all, and, for instance, the wool from Weardale (a great quilting district) is said to be much too harsh. The Rural Industries

Bureau urged the use of wool in quilts made for their marketing scheme, but no suitable supply could be found in the North and it was sent from South Wales to quilters in County Durham. They returned to wadding after the close of the Bureau's scheme.

In South Wales wool seems to have been considered too valuable for use in ordinary quilts, except by those who had their own source of supply. Mrs. Lewis of Llanarth, for instance, preferred to use it and always kept some from her own lambs and used to card it (with her fingers) in the evenings, to avoid wasting daylight. Mrs. Thomas's uncle, who worked in a blanket mill, brought home wool combings for the quilts. I was told in Pembrokeshire that old people would go round the fields collecting wool from the hedges to take with their material to the quilter, buying more from a farmer if they hadn't gathered enough. I doubt whether this was a common practice, for anyone who tries it will find that it takes a great deal of walking, or a number of years, to gather the two or three pounds needed, and then many hours of persistent work to free it of rubbish and dirt. Several Welsh quilters who always used wool said that they had no difficulty in getting it from local farmers.

An old blanket was a popular padding in Wales and was sometimes used in the north of England, where I have also heard of one cover being quilted on to a new blanket, making a quilt of only two layers, having only one "right" side. A Welsh quilter used worn blankets which had originally been made from her own sheep's wool. Sometimes wadding was laid in over the blanket, to make the quilted pattern stand up better. A certain very rough quilter said firmly that only winter quilts had a blanket filling; summer quilts were interlined with two old sheets: another told me that a "best" quilt, with sateen covers, would be padded with cotton-wool and two sheets, and a Westmorland woman said that sheets were used with old blankets. Mrs. Beatrice Scott, a Northumberland woman, wrote in *The Craft of Quilting*[1] that an old blanket and an old sheet would be put aside with pieces of print for making a quilt. Others have spoken of putting muslin, "pieces

[1] *The Craft of Quilting*, by Beatrice Scott. Dryad Press, 1935.

90

ot old pinafores'' or cheesecloth on each side of cotton-wool padding. Sheets and other cotton materials can hardly have added to the warmth of the quilt, so presumably only weight was aimed at. Muslin has sometimes been used over dark-coloured sheep's wool to prevent it from showing through a thin silk material.

Sheep's wool is sometimes used in the form of *domette*, a manufactured woollen lining material. It is expensive, but has all the advantages of wool without any trouble in preparation and is excellent for interlining dressing gowns and other garments, or any quilted work in which the utmost lightness and warmth are of prime importance. Certain other lining materials made of vegetable fibre have been tried but they have various drawbacks and nothing to recommend them in preference to cotton-wool or wadding. Medicated (surgical) cotton-wool should never be put into a quilt because, having been treated to make it absorbent, it would tend to take up any dampness from the atmosphere and would be very difficult to dry after washing.

The fact that quilting had become a thrift craft by means of which the very poorest households could sleep warm is illustrated by the use of rags for padding in South Wales. "The quilt was the ragman," wrote Mrs. A. E. Evans of Carmarthenshire. "Everything that could not be worn any longer was washed, unpicked and pressed and then put in the quilt, fitting every piece tidy, and remember not to have any lumps. Then old sheets or old blankets." Others have mentioned pieces of old clothing and woollen stockings split open, and shirts (probably of Welsh flannel). One family saved all their woollen cast-offs for the village quilter, Mari Panteg; the seams were cut out and it was pressed and used in three layers, and "very hard it was to sew through," as Mari's apprentice remembers! I can hardly bear to think of the annual wash day for these quilts; the wet weight of this conglomeration must have been appalling!

For stitching these thick and heavy quilts stout linen thread or strong cotton (No. 10 or No. 20) had to be used, and one old quilter is described as rubbing her thread with beeswax, like a cobbler!

91

Many a Welsh quilt in its extreme old age became the padding for a new one. When one considers the amount of work which goes to the making of a quilt, even when it is not closely stitched, and the cheapness of the materials in general use some fifty years ago, it is remarkable that every old Welsh quilter will mention the work of recovering. A few quilters in County Durham, Northumberland and Westmorland also spoke of it, but I think it was not so general there. One Welshwoman even said that print quilts "were recovered many times over, as the surface got worn out." The stitches were unpicked and sometimes the old covers were removed entirely and, with new material, or a freshly made piece of patchwork, the quilt was re-made. Only the padding was saved, at the cost of immense labour. One Welshwoman considered this worth doing for a blanket but not for wadding.

In the North Country the old quilt was more often used, as it was, for padding, two new covers being put over it and quilted; this must have been very tough sewing! I have seen one which merely had a new top cover sewn in a simple pattern of stitching which did not go right through, so that the original pattern showed on the underside. A Northumberland woman machines the new covers on in a very simple design. In any case, quilters generally disliked the job of re-covering and many spoke of it as unprofitable; the payment seems to have been the same as for making a new quilt, which was much less laborious. It is difficult to understand why any quilter ever undertook the more complicated kind of re-covering (un-picking the original stitching), unless it was to oblige regular customers from whom more profitable orders could also be expected. The fact that it was done so often in Wales is evidence of the value of all materials and the constant need for thrift in those homes.

One reads occasionally in articles on quilting that thistledown was used as padding. I have never heard of this from any *quilter*, but I was told by someone who was intrigued by the idea, and started to collect thistledown, that after she had assiduously gathered it throughout one summer, she had a bag of dry material which was very heavy though it had shrunk to small bulk, and had no fluffiness or resilience. Thistledown in fact is quite a different sort of substance from cotton-wool and I doubt whether it was ever used to pad quilts. The "twisted silk" used to pad the quilted haketon of Froissart's knight (see above, page 2) may have been specially suitable for protection in battle. I have not found any other mention of its use.

II THE COVERS

Surviving eighteenth-century quilts are of satin, silk or linen or, occasionally, cotton. Quilts with red lutestring lining and "lindsey back" are heard of in the eighteenth century and quilts of "redd sylke" and of "changeable" and black and white silk and "yellowe sercnet" are recorded in the sixteenth century (see Appendix I), but these were the more aristocratic members of their race. The ordinary farmhouse or cottage quilt, doubtless used until it fell to pieces, must have been of homespun woollen or linen or the mixture of these called linsey-woolsey, until imported calico and, later, printed cotton materials became cheap enough for general use. The oldest farmhouse quilts which I have found, made towards the end of the eighteenth or early in the nineteenth century, are of thick, rough homespun, vegetable dyed in dark colours, or of cotton patchwork with a plain underside. Even when wool was no longer spun and woven at home in the sheep-farming districts, "stuff quilts" of cloth or flannel remained popular throughout the nineteenth century. A Carmarthenshire quilter, born in 1871, recalled that cloth woven in the local mills of wool sent in by neighbouring farmers was popular for quilts in her youth, in two colours such as rose or blue with maroon. Some used "French merino bought in the shop" and, later, sateen. Other Welsh quilters mentioned flannel "made and dyed for the purpose" in some of the numerous small woollen mills, and printed flannel or "flannel hand print" and also cashmere. The coarseness of some of the material used may be judged from the fact that an old quilter who worked for farmers described some of the Welsh cloth which was provided for her to quilt as "a bit rough on the hands." It was the general rule to have different colours for the top and the under cover, and the Welsh delighted in strong colours such as red, magenta, maroon, dark blue, green, purple, brown and even black. A County Durham club quilter used contrasting borders on her stuff quilts. "We were always trying to choose materials which stood washing without losing colour," said a Welshwoman, for the household quilts were washed each year in spring, and hung out to dry on a windy day. When nearly dry they were thoroughly shaken out, to make the padding fluff up again.

Various cotton materials were in use about the middle of the last century, generally of a stout, hard-wearing kind, such as calico and "Italian twilled cloth." Calico was sometimes dyed at home (generally red) for one side of the quilt. Turkey twill or "Turkey red" was very popular, and so was "Paisley," which had a red ground and patterns chiefly in yellow. Cotton prints, known in Wales as "stamp," in all colours, particularly lilac, pink and blue, and flowered chintz, were often used, sometimes with white or brown calico for the back. "Lilac print with Turkey red twill borders" was one surprising mixture. Generally the delicate colours seem to have been less popular, perhaps because some were not fast and after several washings faded to a dirty white. Old quilters remember buying these materials at fivepence or sixpence a yard. Towards the end of the century sateens became very popular, "in the grandest colours" as one Welshwoman said, or sometimes figured or flowered. Flowered chintz or sateen, in strong bright colours, was often chosen for wedding quilts in Wales. This vogue for brightly coloured, big, sprawling patterns is odd because the quilted design was lost on them, though it could be seen on the plain stuff generally used on the reverse side. A County Durham woman remembers that her mother would try to persuade her customers to choose plain rather than flowered sateen, so that her quilting would show up better, but most quilters seem not to have been troubled about this. I think it was this use of strongly patterned materials, together with the low rates of payment, which brought the technique of quilting to such a low state in South Wales. In County Durham Mrs. Fletcher tells me she has noticed that the sewing is generally much better on old quilts made in the country districts than in those

36 Quilt by Mrs. Armstrong, Northumberland, who says she got the
idea of the centre pattern from one marked by Elizabeth Sanderson. The
shells and hearts alternating around the feather star, the true lovers' knot
in the middle and the feather hammock used, with these same units, in the
border, are well-known traditional patterns

37 A characteristic Welsh quilt by Mrs. Katy Lewis, Glamorgan, one of
the younger generation of Welsh quilters. Units include leaves, roses (in
outer border and around the centre) and wine-glass

38 Pink and white patchwork quilt made by Mary E. Carr at Blyth,
Northumberland, late nineteenth century, and owned by her daughter,
Mrs. Grays Brown. Though the quilted pattern corresponds to the general
lay-out of the patchwork there is no attempt to keep the stitching within
the shape of the patches Patterns include the bellows (as border),
fans and star

39 Patchwork quilt in baskets pattern, made by Mrs. Armstrong, Northumberland, for the wedding of her daughter, Mrs. Snaith. The quilting fits into the patches and the patterns include clematis and grapes, signifying plenty and prosperity

from the pit villages—where flowered sateens and quilt clubs flourished. When the quilted design was almost lost to view in a riot of colours, it is not surprising that quilters became careless about the drawing and the sewing, especially when working against time for a very few shillings.

In the latter part of the nineteenth century what is generally known in the North as a "strippy" or "stripped" (i.e. striped) quilt became popular in both districts. Two contrasting materials were split lengthways and seamed together to make a top cover with about seven stripes. Turkey red and white were popular, or flowered print and white calico, and later sateen in two plain colours, such as pink and brown, or plain and flowered.

Patchwork in great variety was used for the top covers of quilts throughout the nineteenth century. Some of it was strictly utilitarian, made of every scrap of material available, old or new, joined together in large rectangles for both sides of the quilt. As one old Welsh quilter said, old pieces of cloth padded with rags made a cheap quilt for the farm-servants' beds; in fact it cost nothing but the price of a few reels of cotton and the labour of piecing and quilting—which must have been considerable, but labour was cheap. Mrs. H. E. Lewis in Wales used cloth cuttings from her two brothers, who were tailors; tailors' cuttings, including pieces of flannel and cloth and even tweed, made in the local mills, were mentioned by others in Wales. Mrs. E. Black in County Durham also spoke of stuff quilts made from tailors' pieces. Quilts made of cloth pieces were remembered in Westmorland as being very heavy, but people who were used to them wouldn't sleep under anything else. A Cumberland woman remembered that her mother bought cloth samples from a firm at Warwick Bridge and made them up in handsome patchwork in patterns such as the American Flag (see below) in red and black. Welsh quilters spoke of buying woollen pieces by the pound from a Bradford firm. Stuff quilts made of old material (more common in Wales than in the North) were apt to be dingy, but Welsh flannel in bright red helped to cheer the effect. A typical quilt seen in Wales had an old red shawl with Paisley border as its centre, pieces of black flannel added all round, and squares of red flannel in the corners; pieces of dark-coloured flannel formed the underside. The bought pieces yielded brighter effects; red, blue and green cashmere patchwork was remembered by one old lady, and brown, red, green and purple cloth by another.

There was cotton patchwork also, made of old pieces. "Nothing was ever cast away; everything washed clean and used again"; often the result was just a hotchpotch, or "crazy work" as they called it in the North, though some workers arranged the colours to form a rough pattern. One used "generally a red centre with bright colours round"; others would pick out pieces of two colours only for each quilt.

Large pieces of beautiful—and no doubt precious—chintz were joined together in the same way, backed with white or natural linen, padded and stitched to make lovely quilts, such as two owned by members of the Griffith family in South Wales. The older one was made by a certain Elizabeth Griffith at Pointz Castle in Pembrokeshire in 1770, of pink and blue flowered chintzes, and has always been bequeathed, through several generations, to an Elizabeth in the family. The other, of later date, has fawn as the predominant colour.

Mosaic patchwork, of small pieces cut with templates to geometric shapes, mainly hexagons, lozenges and triangles, was also made in Wales, perhaps when the scraps of material were dressmaker's cuttings too small for use in any other way. I have seen one, for instance, made by Mari Panteg, about 1850, of cotton prints, lilac, pink and blue, arranged in an elaborate design of borders and centre, with white calico on the underside, but one of Mari's former assistants told me that her patchwork was more usually formed of large pieces, and backed with brown calico. There were cuttings from silk gowns, too, such as those used by Mrs. Bowen's mother (see p. 15), and some people bought "silk spares" from Macclesfield for their smartest quilts. Pieces of material are still sold in some Welsh markets, for instance at Maes-teg, for a few pence the pound, for use in patchwork.

Whilst the rectangular style in large pieces was the general characteristic of Welsh patchwork during the last century, the northern counties of England produced a great variety of handsome patterns made up of smaller shapes. A simple form is seen on many "strippy" quilts, which have bands of patchwork in blue, pink, lilac or yellow prints alternating with bands of plain or figured material; for instance, pink print patchwork with white calico between, or blue diamonds and white triangles making up the strips and yellow print between, or diamonds of various cotton prints with strips of lilac between. The patched strips are usually made up of triangles (called half-squares), lozenges (diamonds) and squares.

Many variations of the straight patchwork stripe make effective quilts characteristic of the northern counties; the popular quilting pattern known as *bellows* (seen in the border of Fig. 38) was cut out in two colours and the pieces fitted together alternately; it needed careful drawing and cutting, but no material was wasted. Zigzags, made up of diamond patches, running diagonally across a quilt, and other varieties of broken stripes, are often found, and a pattern called by some the *American flag* (15) was popular in red, blue or green on white. Another simple but effective patchwork pattern is shown in Fig. 34 and a rather more elaborate one in Fig. 38. The border pattern in the last, the *tree of life*, is also found as a single patchwork stripe running up the centre of a quilt. On an American quilt illustrated in Ruth Finley's book it is called *tree everlasting*. Fig. 12 shows the *red star* quilt made by Miss Sanderson (famous as a "stamper") which was a popular pattern in various colours; the white star, each point of the red star, and each border strip is cut out in one piece. Mrs. Fletcher told me that her grandmother in County Durham used it on many quilts, in red and dark green for the boys' beds. Another good all-over patchwork pattern is made up of squares divided into eight triangles of alternate red and white, alternating with plain white squares. Cumberland quilts are said always (within living memory) to have been of patchwork or applied work; the *American flag*, a small star pattern and various others were seen in the Penrith district. Westmorland quilts also show much patchwork, though white, coloured and striped quilts were also found. Mosaic patchwork making up the whole top cover of the quilt was also used in the North and several examples seen showed a good sense of colour, with effective use of white.

Fig. 39 shows one of the favourite patterns—*baskets*—which was also popular in America. Here it is most commonly seen in red and white, but the example illustrated has pink baskets on a yellow ground; the quilter who made it for her daughter's wedding said disapprovingly. "She had what she wanted but I didna' like the colours mysel'." The handles of the baskets are cut out in one piece and applied. I saw a quilt in Weardale on which the baskets themselves (forty-two of them) are all applied. The most striking applied work (40) is on a quilt belonging to Mrs. Cruddas of Rookhope, Weardale, and was made by her husband's great grandmother. This beautiful pattern, in Turkey red and green prints on white, is of a type generally believed to be found only in America. A Northumberland quilt which was spoken of as something very special (but was not seen) was described as patched with feathers in green twill on white. The pieced or applied work on many American quilts is based on *quilting* patterns well known here, such as *wine-glass* (American versions are called *melon patch*, and *orange peel*) and *feather ring*, and the Victoria and Albert Museum's *Notes on Applied Work and Patchwork* shows (Plate 13) a *running feather* border pattern in patchwork.

A Cumberland coverlet made in the first half of the nineteenth century has five "plate" motifs (more like oblong angular dishes) of flowered chintz applied on white, in the centre, and four borders of variegated patchwork, finished with a border of black and brown print. This was quilted, without any padding, in a simple *dogs' teeth* pattern, on calico. In the same county a patchwork quilt made up of white squares bordered with blue had six "pennies" of various colours applied with buttonhole stitch in a ring round a seventh central one on each square; one of these squares had originally been sent from Canada and copied. Another piece of applied work which had crossed the Atlantic was found in Pembrokeshire, a flower-pot pattern in red and green prints on white, made by the owner's great aunt and sent home to be quilted about a hundred years ago. This type of work, not unusual in the North (compare Mrs. Cruddas's quilt, mentioned above), seems to have been unknown in Wales and was not, apparently, imitated there.

Most of the patchwork and applied work described above (except the two Griffith quilts) was made since the middle of the nineteenth century. One earlier piece, of outstanding interest, certainly made before 1826, is "Old Joe's" quilt (11) in which the patchwork is composed partly of small patches, partly of large squares and strips. The large centre-piece of a flower basket and wreath, and the heraldic corners, are probably printed squares which were made and sold specially for use in patchwork. The palm tree and pheasant squares were cut from an eighteenth-century print made in imitation of Indian prints. Joe's customers may have supplied him with the materials from which he pieced their quilts.

Some people in Northumberland described the "old quilts" as having been mostly patched in big squares, oblongs or stars; one had a Paisley square in the centre and blue all round (which sounds like Wales). But the evidence suggests, on the whole, that all kinds of patchwork persisted throughout the nineteenth century in Northumberland, Cumberland, Westmorland, County Durham and Yorkshire, and that it was usually made as the top cover for a quilt. Several quilters spoke of how they used to sit patching at nights; scraps of print left over from dresses were all saved for patchwork, pieces of print were bought from a firm in Leeds at one shilling and a penny for a hundred, or swotches from a Newcastle shop. Mrs. Bell of Greenhead remembers that women came from Carlisle with big baskets of remnants of cotton print to sell and her mother never turned them away. The bigger pieces were torn in strips for strippy quilts (like the pieces left over from bondagers' overalls, mentioned by Beatrice Scott) and the smaller ones cut into patches. In a Westmorland village I heard of a man who cut out the patches for his mother's quilts and sometimes sewed them together. Mrs. Whitwell, in the same county, told how her uncle, a Yorkshire cobbler, made many patchwork quilts for himself and members of his family, cutting out the hexagonal pieces with a penknife on his last, joining them and quilting them in a simple pattern, following the shape of the pieces.

There were probably some quilts made in the North, particularly the stuff quilts of tailors' pieces, as crude as those which are so plentiful in Wales, but generally the standard of patchwork is much higher in the North and perhaps for that reason the less carefully patched quilts were not brought out to show. Again, a higher standard of living in the North is indicated; people there could buy their pieces of print in sufficient quantity to choose the colours wanted. Patchwork was treated as an art, it must be carefully planned, cut and sewn to give a decorative effect; it was not merely a means of making good use of every old scrap of material.

I have studied patchwork in the North only incidentally, as it turned up in connection with quilting; what I found by accident suggests that a great deal more is stored in the farmhouses and cottages. "I maun gae to the kist for it," said one old lady looking for a quilt to show me, and many other kists must hold similar treasure. I find worthy of record a quilter's dramatic description of a neighbour finishing a piece of patchwork: "She loosed the papers and dashed it and all the papers cam oot." I have illustrated one quilt which, strictly speaking, has no place in this book; Figs. 41 and 43 show an interesting and unusual form of patchwork in a small red and white calico coverlet; the hexagonal patches are gathered tightly by several running threads and attached to an interlining to keep them in place, the whole backed with a loose white lining. Considerable skill must have been used to construct this piece of work; it is not quilted and hardly could be, but its peculiar texture gives it a rich appearance, comparable to the effect of quilting.

Although a considerable amount of patchwork is done nowadays I have not seen any in the simple two-colour traditional patterns which are so worthy of revival. Quilting certainly enhances their appearance by an added richness of texture, but unquilted they are still handsome. Turkey twill is still to be bought, and reasonably good substitutes for other coloured prints, if genuine old pieces cannot be found. The finished work has a character of its own; without the intricacy of mosaic patchwork (which generally involves the collection of a multitude of scraps) or of the often over-elaborate American pieced work, it has an effective simplicity and naive charm.

III MATERIALS USED TODAY

The best material for quilts is closely woven, soft and smooth, with a slightly lustrous surface, so that it reflects enough light to show up the pattern clearly. The old-fashioned sateen was excellent and so was the fine cotton poplin which was used for many quilts made under the Rural Industries Bureau's scheme between 1929 and 1939. Cotton or linen materials which have not a glossy surface, although they were much used in the past, do not show the quilted pattern to the best advantage; they are most effective in white or pale colours. Shiny rayon materials are often used, with lamentable effect. They have too many highlights, which give the quilt a spotty look, breaking up the flowing lines of the pattern and disguising it. Many of them, also, are too wiry to be suitable for quilting. But it is possible to find a rayon silk, only slightly lustrous, which can be effectively quilted. Real silk is beautiful when quilted; it was much used in the eighteenth century, and satin too, but they are too expensive for most occasions. Velvet is difficult for the quilter to mark and to work on—"the pattern wouldna' bide on" one of them complained—but it has been quilted successfully, as a house-gown, though the result is slightly blurred, lacking that clear-cut effect which is characteristic of the best quilted work.

Any material for quilting should of course be good enough to stand long wear; otherwise it is not worthy of the amount of sewing which would be put into it. If it is washable, so much the better, because a quilt, especially if padded with wool, can be washed many times without harm. In fact the wash tub may hold less danger than the dry-cleaning process because any method of cleaning by suction tends to draw the padding out through the material and the quilt returns thinner but with a fine growth of hair all over it!

Patterned materials, as has been said, were much used for nineteenth-century quilts, but that was a fashion which seems to be deservedly dead, so far as the big bold patterns are concerned. Small sprigged patterns can be quite pretty when quilted, but give the quilter a new difficulty if she is to treat them in relation to her own design.

The criteria by which the suitability of a material for quilting should be judged are: (i) Can the quilter work on it comfortably? (ii) Will it show the quilted pattern to the greatest effect and in its full beauty? and (iii) Will it last? A material is not necessarily unsuitable because it has never been used before, any more than it is suitable because it *has* been used; nowadays silk and cotton and rayon textiles are continually being produced in new versions, and some completely new textiles appear. The craftswoman, if she is not misled by the smart appearance of some glossy stuff used for quite a different purpose, should be able to judge what is most suitable to set up in her frame.

40 White quilt with applied pattern in Turkey red and green prints
Quilted with five borders, chain and worm patterns alternating, and dia-
monds in centre with a border of stars Piped edges. Made by Isabella
Cruddas at Rookhope, County Durham, about 1850; owned by Mrs
Martha M. Cruddas

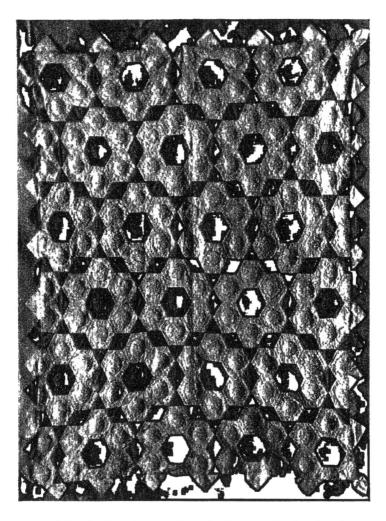

41 Red and white calico coverlet made of groups of gathered patches
joined by flat triangular and rhomboid patches Made by Isabella Cruddas at
Rookhope, County Durham, about 1850, owned by Mrs Martha M.
Cruddas (See also Fig 43)

CHAPTER SIX

The Patterns

"IT is a lovely work," said one old Welshwoman, "and very interesting to see your patterns form under your hand." The patterns are the important, the vital, feature of quilting, but there are many misconceptions current about them, due partly to generalizations which have been made from too little evidence. The patterns are traditional, but this word is so often misused nowadays that it may convey the wrong idea, the idea of something static, carefully preserved from the past like a mummy or a fly in amber, no longer having any life of its own. The *Oxford (Pocket) Dictionary* tells us that tradition is "the oral transmission of knowledge or belief from one generation to another; the body of such knowledge etc., so transmitted." Knowledge which is handed down by word of mouth is bound to undergo some changes from generation to generation and also there will be many streams of it, each with its own variations, in the many lines of transmission (generally families in the case of quilting). There can be nothing rigidly standardized, nothing definitely fixed, in traditional knowledge, so long as the tradition is *living*. We have not a great deal of living tradition in this country; much of our traditional art, such as folk songs and dances, was rescued from extinction at a time when only a few old people still held the knowledge of it; it was noted and recorded by outsiders, not by the people to whom it would naturally have been passed on in the ordinary course of tradition. And so it became fixed in the form in which it was recorded and is no longer liable to that constant change and development which oral tradition undergoes.

Thus many people think of "traditional pattern" as something which has been settled once for all and ought not to be changed.

The knowledge of quilting, however, is still a living tradition; a great many of the people who practise it today have inherited it from their mothers and have added to it their own ideas and variations, as others had done before them. Therefore the tradition cannot be formulated in exact rules and anyone trying to do so does a great disservice to the craft by attempting to cramp its natural growth. Every pattern had its first appearance at some time and, to those who value our native traditions, that fertility of invention of quilting design, which is so noticeable in South Wales, and less so in the north of England, today, is a sign of triumphant life. The criterion of a pattern should be: "Is it right? Does it look right? Has it the characteristics of a good traditional quilting pattern?" One of the few things which it is safe to stigmatize as *wrong* is a pattern taken from a "transfer" or other design for embroidery, because it has been designed (often not well designed, at that) for another form of needlework with different requirements. The quilting pattern depends in the main, not so much upon its lines of stitching as upon the shapes which those lines enclose and which stand up in relief. Embroidery patterns have sometimes been used, mistakenly, by quilters, particularly for cushions for which they often find difficulty in adapting their large quilt designs, but their wrongness can be seen immediately; they have a poor, scratchy look instead of the bold sculptural effect of quilting. Relief carving may suggest a good quilt pattern, such as the *Tudor rose* (42), which probably came from such a source. A quilter may also find a pattern in wrought ironwork, because that depends upon good, simple line and upon the background seen through the thin metal bars. A cut-glass tumbler was another source of inspiration. Many patterns are based on leaves and flowers, particularly in Wales (44, 45), but these generally need to be formalized. A naturalistic spray variously described as a *basket of flowers, bowl of roses, vase of flowers* or *flower pot* is found on many old Welsh quilts and some North Country ones, and Mrs.

Hake[1] notes that it is a characteristic centrepiece in West Country quilts. Flower and leaf patterns of this type, similar in style to contemporary embroidery designs, were much used on eighteenth-century petticoats (Plate 9 in *Notes on Quilting*[2] shows one of the more formal type, and Plate 15 another) and evidently remained in favour everywhere throughout the nineteenth century, but they are more difficult to use than the conventional patterns, and on some old North Country quilts the effect is so confused that it cannot be shown clearly in a photograph. Applied versions are well shown in Fig. 40.

It is often said that North Country patterns are flowing and Welsh patterns geometric. The latter are "strongly reminiscent of the days of the Vikings," according to one highly imaginative writer, and others have mentioned a Phoenician origin, but no evidence was produced to support these theories, which are nonsense. Welsh quilting in the past fifty years has certainly tended towards patterns with a centre-piece, generally square or round, and one or more borders enclosed in rectangular frames (37, 48 and 49), whereas a type of pattern with few or no rectangular border lines has been very popular in the North; Figs. 1, 36 and 47 show characteristic patterns from the North. But a great many North Country quilts of the nineteenth century show designs on similar lines to those usually called Welsh (3, 51 and also 34, 38). The quilted patterns on these last two were obviously dictated by the patches and I think that the nineteenth-century popularity of patchwork and also of the "strippy" quilt must have had its influence on the quilted patterns. When strips of materials of two colours are used for a quilt, the pattern is usually arranged in corresponding strips, and border patterns were used a great deal and developed in many ways. The *running feather* (46), so popular in County Durham nowadays and used in Northumberland also, is often found singly on a "strippy" quilt. *Twist, worm,* many kinds of *chain, plait, bellows and star,* were all used on the strips.

1 *English Quilting Old and New,* by Elizabeth Hake. B. T. Batsford Ltd.
2 *Notes on Quilting,* Victoria and Albert Museum. H.M. Stationery Office.

Probably no pattern, unless it is of very recent origin, can be positively assigned to any particular county or district. The very formal tight feather pattern is generally considered as typical of County Durham, but Plate 27 in Mrs. Hake's book shows a Devonshire version of the *feather ring* and Plates 14 and 15 another, older, Devonshire feather in looser style, similar to the Northumbrian one of similar date (6) and to many others on eighteenth-century petticoats (locality unknown) in the Victoria and Albert Museum. A similar pattern used in Wales is generally known as the *fern*.

Patterns may now spread far and wide through photographs reproduced in books and periodicals, through quilts shown in national exhibitions (such as those held by the National Federation of Women's Institutes) and through quilts sold to distant customers. Any of these may be seen by quilters far from where the quilt was made, who may carry home a mental picture of some shape and reproduce it later. But no good quilter would try to memorize and copy the design of the whole quilt. All quilt designs are built up of pattern units; for instance, Fig. 49 shows a design made up of *wine-glass, shell, diamonds, roses* and *fans*. A quilter with only a comparatively small repertory of patterns can combine them in an infinite variety of designs, but she may always be ready to borrow a new one. Even before photography was invented or national exhibitions of handicrafts were thought of, patterns could travel. The movement of country people to the industrial districts in the nineteenth century must have introduced many unfamiliar units to the quilters of the Glamorgan valleys and the Durham and Northumberland pit villages. Mrs. Lace of Aberdare told me that when she began to quilt for a living in 1907 her patterns were derived from her paternal grandmother, who came from Somerset, and her mother, whose family had come in the previous generation from Scotland; but as she worked at her frame, and therefore took more interest in local quilting, she "was picking up Welsh patterns all the time." Mrs. Hitchcock's mother from Cleveland, Yorkshire, taught her daughter in County Durham the *running feather*, the *feather ring* for a centre and other feather patterns. Mrs. William Hodgson's mother, also from the East

42 Centre of a quilt by Mrs. D. K. Walters, Glamorgan, with Tudor
rose and other patterns

43 Detail of coverlet shown in Fig. 41

44 Quilt by Mrs D K Walters, Glamorgan. The pattern combines
many traditional units, including flower and leaf shapes and sea waves,
fans, Paisley pears and roses

45 Quilt made in the 1930's by a young Welsh girl, Miss G. K. Evans
(now Mrs. Boundy) The pattern combines variations on traditional units
with new ideas and shows great fertility of invention

46 Running
feather pattern
with feather-
wreath border

47 Both the
above are typi-
cal of County
Durham work
since about
1930

Riding of Yorkshire, used the *running feather*. but only worked "up and down" patterns; those with centrepieces Mrs. Hodgson learnt in County Durham.

From the illustrations and descriptions in the three books dealing with American quilts already mentioned it would seem that a number of well-known English and Welsh patterns crossed the Atlantic and have been used there again and again. Various feather patterns, including *ring*, *wreath* and *running*

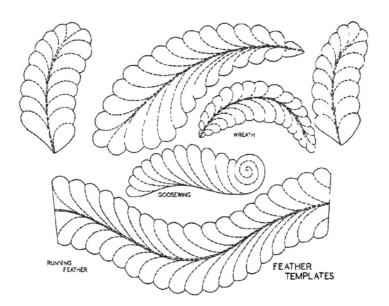

feather, several versions of the *twist* (called *rope*), *wine-glass* (called *teacup quilting*) the *rose* or *whorl* and of course *diamonds* (called *crossbar quilting*), were evidently popular, and there is a version of the *vase of roses* called *bouquet*.

Marriage quilts must have travelled a little in the old days from their place of origin, especially those made for the daughter of the great house, who was more likely than the cottagers to marry away from her place of birth; but even the humbler families did move sometimes and their quilts went with them as a precious part of the household goods. Once the housewife was settled in her new home and able to set up her quilt frame, her neighbours would certainly be interested in any unfamiliar patterns she might use and before long they would be begging the loan of a template.

There are many pattern units in common use in all the districts where quilting is still done and some of these are seen, too, on the old West Country quilts and on older specimens in museums. Such are the *fan*, many feather, flower, leaf and spray patterns, and the background patterns, *wine-glass, shell* and *diamonds*. Curiously enough the *twist*, which must be one of the oldest patterns in the Western world since it is common on Roman mosaics, is not often seen on seventeenth- or eighteenth-century work, though it appears with the *plait* on a Portuguese "stuffed" quilt illustrated in the Victoria and Albert Museum's *Notes* and on a very early nineteenth-century Monmouthshire quilt. A variation of it was used by "Old Joe" in Northumberland (see page 129) and by Elizabeth Griffith in Pembrokeshire in 1770. It has been so widely used during the last hundred years or so that it must surely have been in many quilters' repertories long before.

Since the patterns have been handed down in families it is not surprising that there are endless variations of them and many names for the same pattern, and also—still more confusing— one name may be used in different families or different districts to describe different patterns. For instance, *twist* is also called *trail* or *dog trail, chain, lost chain, rope*, or, in the northernmost part of Northumberland, *English chain*. Nowadays it is often called *cable*, but I believe this to be a modern name. Some people only call it *chain* when its lines cross instead of going over and under, though this version may also be called *trail* or *plait*, but *plait* generally means a real plait, which may alternatively be called *difficult chain*. *Chain* may also mean the simple twist pattern sometimes known as *spectacles* (see page 81).

The ubiquitous *diamonds* are generally drawn square, not diamond-shaped, both in old and modern work, but they can be—and sometimes are—made diamond-shape with the usual templates, as is shown on page 80, and in my eyes this is a more elegant version. *Diamonds* are known in Wales as *plaid* or *plaiding* and sometimes as *trellis*, but others use this name only for *double diamonds*, in which they are drawn with double lines, as is seen on an eighteenth-century petticoat (2) and a modern Welsh quilt (50). *Mother of thousands* is a picturesque alternative name for the *shell* background pattern; the name *shell* is also used for several other shapes.

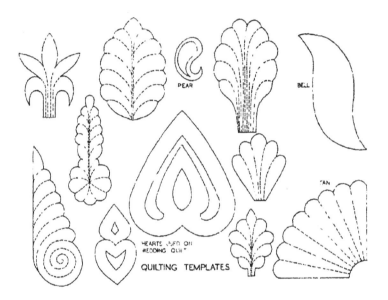

QUILTING TEMPLATES

There are many other instances of the complicated and contradictory naming of patterns. It suggests that pattern names are traditional in families but were not generally passed from one quilter to another outside the family, except perhaps when several worked together. Many quilters have said that they have no names for some of the patterns they used: "Mother didn't christen them," said one; the Misses Johnson said that their mother often referred to a pattern by some such name as "Betty Jamieson's thing," naming the friend whose template she had borrowed. In recent years some alien names have crept in; it sometimes happened that people at the London end of the Rural Industries Bureau's scheme, trying to explain to a quilter the pattern wanted and not knowing the local name, gave it one of their own; the worker often adopted this with surprising alacrity. Once when I asked a County Durham woman if the name she used, which struck me as rather highfalutin (I think it was *Roman armour* for the filling usually called *shell*), was an old name, she answered: "Oh no, but the ladies in London like it"!

The names of many pattern units suggest that they were copied from common objects; there are the *plait, chain, hour-glass, pair of scissors, bellows, plate, basin, flat iron, hammock, bell, goose wing, coxcomb, fan, shell, dogs' teeth, worm, "sheff of corn"*, and many others, as well as the various *ferns, roses, leaves* and *stars*, and the popular *feather* in its many forms. In a few cases the pattern is certainly named from the template used; some instances were mentioned on page 49. Other patterns, such as *cord and tassels*, also called *hammock, festoon* or *cap peak* (see p.81) and *fan* (p.119), are simplified drawings of the objects named. Some patterns, such as *scissors* (the bottom left-hand template on p.119), seem to have only a remote resemblance to their namesake and may have been designed in the first place as a shape to fill a space and afterwards named from a supposed likeness. *Dogs' teeth*, a simple zigzag, like the Norman dog-tooth moulding, may have been so called from this architectural resemblance, but its name was more likely an independent idea. "Mother despised dogs' teeth," said Miss Johnson. A Northumberland woman, seeing the ogee pattern on the eighteenth-century work shown in Fig. 6, said "It's like rigs in a field" (the ridges of ploughed land). *Rigs* is a good name, but no one knows whether the first designer of this pattern (which is frequently found, with several variations, on petticoats of that period, but seems to have gone out of use) ever had ploughland in mind. An instance of a new unit designed in Northumberland in this century from a common object is given by Mrs. Bell's mother who, wanting something to fill a space on a quilt, made a template from the clothes brush and used this twice, one shape across the other. Miss Shepherd designed a pattern unit from the embossed leather binding of the family Bible, making a simplified drawing and enlarging it until she was satisfied and could cut the template. The stamped pattern on the wooden seat of an ordinary chair gave her an idea for a new filling in her *shell* template. The moulding on the oven door suggested to Mrs. Davison's mother an effective all-over pattern.

Some of the manifold uses of a round template have already

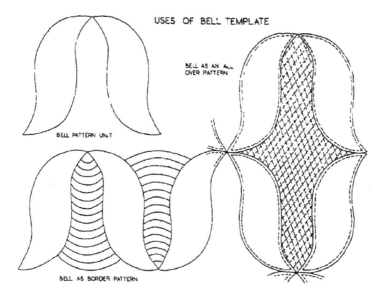

USES OF BELL TEMPLATE

BELL AS AN ALL OVER PATTERN

BELL PATTERN UNIT

BELL AS BORDER PATTERN

been mentioned; the *wine-glass* pattern (also known as *plates* or *wheels*, as well as *cuddy's lug*) may be given quite a different air by a variety of fillings, if it is done on a fairly large scale, such as small squares (not actually diamonds, though they may be so called, see Fig. 37), or little *stars*, or Durham *roses* or Welsh *roses*. The template for the *bell* (see above) gives another good example of various patterns from one simple shape; the single unit is sometimes known as a *tulip* and may be used in a border pattern.

Let us now picture a quilter (not one of those who marks

the whole pattern on the material beforehand) with her quilt set up in the frame, a part—perhaps one-third—of its width spread smoothly, marked only with a few measurements, and the rest rolled up. How does she set about designing her quilt? Everyone has her own method, but it is certainly the general practice of many Welsh quilters, and some North Country ones, to form a mental picture of the design. Miss Emiah Jones of Carmarthenshire, a notable Welsh quilter, once said that her mother was "wonderful at giving her mind-picture of the design she wanted us to do"; father then drew it in chalk on the kitchen flagstones, at her direction. Another Welshwoman told how she woke in the night with the plan for her next quilt in her mind, lighted a candle and sketched it on the wallpaper so that she would not forget it. Mrs. Isabella Fletcher of County Durham, talking of how she designs her quilts, said: "I can sit some hours at the frame before I know where I'm getting with it."

It is unusual for a quilter to draw the design on paper before she starts to mark it on the quilt; I came across one who kept a scrap-book of designs which she had worked or had only thought of or perhaps noted from quilts she had seen, but I think most quilters could reproduce any design once worked without any such record. Although, as one old lady put it, "the last inch must be like the first," a quilter generally has no need to look back at the first section worked to remind herself how it was done. Though the general plan is worked out in her mind before she begins, some details may not be planned until she comes to them; she may tell you: "I'm not quite sure how I'll fill in that space; perhaps I'll put roses, or it might be pears." But when she has stitched it the picture remains clear in her mind until she comes to do the last corresponding piece at the other side of the quilt, and it is reproduced accurately.

For the traditional quilter designing is simply a part of the work of making quilts; she learnt the setting up, the planning, the marking and the sewing from Mother or Grannie and she has never thought of herself as a "designer." This is as it should be (but too often is not, in handicraft today); only so long as this intimate connection between the technique and the design is maintained will the quilting tradition remain alive. There are, of course, good designers and others less good: there are some whose repertory is small and who do not venture beyond slight variations in the arrangement of a limited store of templates, whilst others delight in producing elaborate designs completely different from anything they have done before. The tradition is more fluid in South Wales and the quilters there more adventurous. There is a type of design in Wales which may be considered characteristic and which can be recognized in Figs. 48 and 49, one with a round and one with a square centre. Both these patterns are composed entirely of traditional units arranged in a familiar style. The corners of Mrs. Morgan's quilt are well managed and it is interesting to contrast them with the corners of a similar border on the little homespun quilt shown in Fig. 3, whose maker hardly attempted to solve the problem. Incidentally this is a Northumbrian quilt, but might equally have been made in Wales. Two Welsh cot quilts show original developments of all-over designs used in both areas; Miss Gwen Stone has transformed the familiar overlapping circles (53), and a Merthyr worker has arranged the *sea waves* in a new way (4). Another quilt by Mrs. Irene Morgan (55) shows much originality in its use of traditional units. Miss Jessie Edwards, a supreme mistress of her craft, combines traditional units and original ideas in a design of characteristically Welsh style, great richness and good balance (13). Fig. 56 shows a design of masterly simplicity (including the *pennies*) used on a cot quilt by Miss Emiah Jones, a versatile Carmarthenshire quilter who has taught many others. Fig. 9 is a more elaborate example of her work in which notable points are her original use of small pieces of the *twist* pattern and the new look she has given to the *shell* by outlining it with many close lines of sewing. The *roses* in both these quilts are an interesting feature; this is a spiral pattern and many workers start sewing it in the centre and work round and round in widening circles, but Miss Jones starts on the outer edge and by sewing very close lines makes the centre of the *rose* stand up in a little peak; unorthodox, perhaps, but pretty. The same effect is seen in a quilt by Mrs.

Muriel Davies (57), who was Miss Jones's pupil. Its usual form can be seen in the border of Fig. 57, and in several others.

Several of these quilts mentioned above illustrate the value of contrast in quilt design; it may be the contrast between close lines of sewing and open spaces—note, for instance, in Fig. 13, how Miss Edwards uses treble rows of sewing to mark her *diamonds* and to outline other shapes, and compare the North Country quilts by Mrs. Armstrong and Mrs. Coulthard (36 and 1) with their backgrounds of very small diamonds. Miss Emiah Jones's *pennies* stand out against a background in which very close stitchery gives a stippled effect; a similar effect is seen in the eighteenth-century petticoat (2) and in an early nineteenth-century white American quilt illustrated in Florence Peto's book. Another kind of contrast—between curves and straight lines—is seen in Mrs. Morgan's quilt (55).

The essentials of good quilt design are the same as for any design and might be summarized as balance, contrast and clarity (though there will be many other definitions), combined with suitability for the technique of the craft and for the particular piece of work. (The problems of designing quilted garments and cushions are mentioned in Chapter Seven.) Beyond this it is unsafe to dogmatize—though many quilters will do so. One Welshwoman told me firmly that "there should be a wheel in the centre, with spokes. Some people put a round, with leaves in it, but that's not correct. The rest of the pattern should be made up of borders." This was evidently the tradition in her own family; others, too, have said that a Welsh quilt must always have a ring in the centre, or that it must have three borders. I have even heard that a teacher of quilting has laid it down that every quilt must have three different "filling" (background) patterns. But most quilters have more elastic ideas—fortunately for the development of the craft.

"My patterns are all family patterns" is another common fallacy; they may turn out to consist of some of the most universally found units, *roses, leaves, twist* and so forth. But this

48 Quilt by Mrs Irene Morgan, Glamorgan. The outer border is the church windows pattern Fondness for leaf patterns is perhaps a Welsh characteristic

49   Quilt by Mrs Edgell, Monmouthshire Characteristic Welsh
arrangement of traditional units

50   Quilt by Mrs. Marguerite Nicholas, Glamorgan. The border is a
double version of cord and tassel (popular in the north of England)
Double diamonds are the filling for the central panel

51 Part of quilt made in Elsdon, Northumberland, before 1900,
described by owner, Mrs Telfer, as a typical old-fashioned pattern

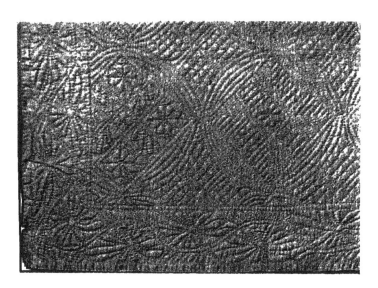

52 Part of an eighteenth-century cradle quilt The border, repeated,
would form the popular bellows and star pattern

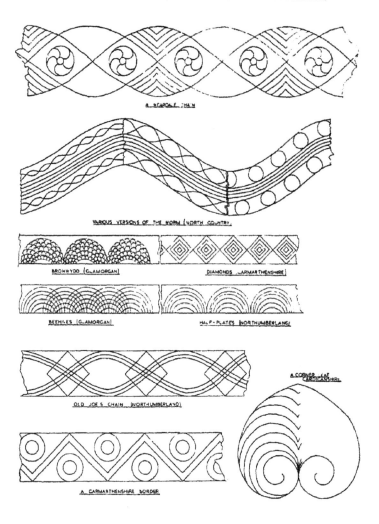

A SEADALE CHAIN

VARIOUS VERSIONS OF THE WORM (NORTH COUNTRY)

BRONWYDD (GLAMORGAN)

DIAMONDS (CARMARTHENSHIRE)

BEEHIVES (GLAMORGAN)

HALF-PLATES (NORTHUMBERLAND)

OLD JOE'S CHAIN (NORTHUMBERLAND)

A CORNER (CARDIGANSHIRE)

A CARMARTHENSHIRE BORDER

harmless family pride is only a version of the "trade secret"
and quilters on the whole are generous with their templates
and their ideas, and generous in their praise of others. "I've

129

got a dumb hand for drawing," said a North Country quilter, "You should see Mrs. W.; she's a fancy-pattern woman."

One can roughly classify North Country quilts of the nineteenth century in three groups. Examples of what are often called the "old-fashioned patterns" are seen in Mrs. Telfer's quilt (51), Mary Carr's quilt (38) and Elizabeth Sanderson's "Red Star" (12); in the last two the plan has been dictated by the patchwork. They are not unlike the Welsh style. Then there were the strippy quilts, with border patterns running the length of the quilt, *twists* and *plaits* in all their variations, *worm* (Diagram, p.81), *running feather, cord and tassels, bellows, waves,* and even small patterns such as *roses* or *shells* arranged in rows. Such quilts were easy to design, with little planning needed and no corners to turn. A very large proportion of the quilts made from about the middle of the nineteenth century until, perhaps, thirty years ago were of this type; seventy-five per cent. was the estimate of a Durham woman with a wide knowledge of quilting in her own county. I think that many quilters learnt only this kind of pattern and so had no skill in turning the corners of a border or in planning a design with a centre. I have seen even a plain white quilt worked in strip patterns, but in South Wales the quilts made up of strips of different coloured materials are, more often than not, quilted in the usual Welsh style with borders and a centre (35).

Possibly it was this predominance of the "strippy" quilt which gave the mysterious Mr. Gardiner his opportunity to originate the third style of nineteenth-century North Country design. Perhaps he was asked to draw the pattern on a quilt top for some local quilter who wanted something more impressive than the strip patterns which were the only kind she was used to. Where this village shopkeeper in the remote district of Allendale got the ideas for his patterns I do not know; he had a good understanding of what would be effective in quilting, a remarkable talent for design and a varied fancy. I have seen several quilts which were marked by him and many which were marked by Miss Sanderson or her apprentices, and although the style is always recognizable I have never seen two identical patterns. Miss Hall's quilt (14) and Mrs. Milburn's quilt, marked and sewed by Miss Humble (5), are typical examples. Many traditional units are used; there is always, so far as I know, a background of very small diamonds, and there is a great deal of elaborate freehand filling. These patterns may be considered too complicated, but they have a very rich effect.

Miss Sanderson probably started her apprenticeship about 1875, and presumably Mr. Gardiner had then been drawing quilt tops for some time to have become so well known and to have so many orders that he could afford to take a pupil; Miss Sanderson in her prime could draw two quilt tops in a day, so the output, even when she started, must have been considerable. I have heard of seven "stampers" who were apprenticed to Miss Sanderson or to her pupils, and there may have been more. This school of design which started so unpretentiously in the hamlet of Dirt Pot spread to immense proportions and had a remarkable influence on quilt design in Northumberland and Weardale and probably farther afield. Through the medium of the packman and, later, through the local co-operative shops, the marked quilt tops reached the remotest farms and villages. The Misses Johnson in Hexhamshire said that patched or stripped quilts were hand laid (marked by the quilter, with templates), but the best quilts (for which new material would be bought) were "stamped." When the various church quilt clubs in Amble were working hard to raise funds for the War Memorial in 1918 they took a lot of their material to the stores to be sent away to be marked, "otherwise they would never have got them all done in the time," said Mrs. Burton. Some-one else explained that it saved time to buy a marked quilt top, though this is hard to understand since there was so much work in the intricate patterns. In any case, the custom of buying drawn quilt tops, or of sending one's own material away to be marked, spread to such an extent that a number of quilters never learnt to mark a pattern and cannot do so to this day. It also had a stultifying effect on Northumberland and Durham designs. Even if no two of these quilts were exactly alike, many of them have a very strong family resemblance and the general style seems to have remained the same, with few if any innovations, throughout the period of—probably—nearly a hundred years since Mr. Gardiner marked his first quilt top.

Two beautiful quilts made by Mrs. Armstrong (36) and Mrs. Coulthard, Miss Sanderson's first apprentice (1), show that workers who are accustomed to planning their own designs can use a simplified version of this style with good effect. Mrs. Armstrong told me that she got the idea for the centre of her quilt from one which was sent away to be "stamped"; the "old quilts," according to her, were never done in this style, but only in strips. Mrs. Coulthard's centre and corners are the result of Miss Sanderson's influence. On the whole, however, I believe that the influence was an unfortunate one, since the less enterprising quilter either never created her own designs or, at least, confined herself to strip patterns and bought a drawn quilt top when she wanted to do anything grander.

The standardization of what are commonly known as the Durham feather patterns may be partly due to this same mental indolence. There are a number of complete designs for quilts which are produced by a number of workers, either in exactly the same detail or with only the slightest variations. One of them is shown in Fig. 46; the centre is made up of *running feathers* and the border of *feather wreaths* with *roses* in the corners; there is a slight touch of originality in the border line of *pennies*. The *running feathers* were a popular strip pattern and were sometimes worked as shown here, but without any border, as the whole pattern on a plain quilt. Figure 47 illustrates the *rose and shells* centre with *feather ring* round (there are several different patterns called "shell"), and *feather wreaths* in the border with *roses* in the corners; between border and centre, at each end of the quilt, is the *sheff of corn*, with a *pair of scissors* on each side of it. Other names for this corner *rose* are *wheel, wheel of hope, whorl, Catherine wheel* and *boozy Betty*. This particular quilt has a variation from the standard "feather ring and wreaths" pattern in the ingenious arrangement of the corners. It was made to order and evidently the measurements gave the quilter some difficulty, for she could not fit in four wreaths across the ends, and three were not enough. The management of the corners is considered to be one test of a good quilt designer. "Many quilters," said Mrs. Hitchcock, "won't put themselves about to make the feathers run right round the quilt," meaning that when using, for instance, a *running feather* as a border they will break it off at the corners and put in a rose as an easy solution (12).

One of the standard designs using the *feather wreath* and *feather ring* originated in the tiny pit village of Page Bank, where Mrs. Snaith, an old lady from Willingdon, helped to mark the first quilt made co-operatively by members of Page Bank Women's Institute about 1920. Mrs. Snaith gave the *feather wreath* template to one of the quilters, Mrs. Hodgson, and presumably the others took copies of it, for the design was reproduced many times, even after most of the quilters had moved away from Page Bank when the pit there was closed. The "London ladies" who were booking orders for quilts under the Rural Industries Bureau's scheme discovered that they could be worked in this design by at least eight different quilters, all of whom came from Page Bank, and it was therefore called in London the Page Bank pattern.

In Wales there is no comparable standardization of designs, nor this tendency to repeat a whole design exactly. Possibly a quilter working at top speed, for small payment, on club quilts might repeat the very simple designs often used for this kind of work, but I have never seen two Welsh quilts exactly alike except for a few which were made to order as pairs (even in these cases the makers preferred to have some slight difference in detail), and excepting also two copies of an old Somerset quilt which were deliberately made for special reasons. Several Welsh quilters have said sternly: "The same design is never done twice," and this is generally true. At an exhibition of traditional quilting held at the Welsh Folk Museum at St. Fagan's Castle in 1951, for which entries were invited from all over Wales, it was noticeable that all the sixty-five accepted exhibits, of which twenty were large quilts, were completely different in design and the excellence and variety of the work were astonishing.

To what extent can the patterns now generally considered traditional be traced back to seventeenth- and eighteenth-century work? There is no hope of tracing them back further because hardly any quilted work of this type has survived from earlier dates. Even for those two centuries the evidence is scanty and can be but a tiny fraction of all the quilted work that was done. Four quilts of the traditional wadded type are illustrated in the Victoria and Albert Museum's *Notes on Quilting*, and two others from the Museum shown here (10 and 52) were chosen because they show most affinity with modern work. We do not know if both were made by one worker or in one place, but they have the same border pattern and turn the corners in the same way. The *bellows and star* pattern much used in the North today is an extended version of this. The quilt illustrated as Fig. 52 shows the *wine-glass* filling, broken by the diagonal bands; Fig. 10 is similar in general style to much nineteenth-century work, particularly Welsh (cf. Fig. 44). It is noticeable that the centres of both quilts seem to have been marked bit by bit, as the work proceeded, without any attempt to make a section of the pattern fit neatly into the corners. Other details suggestive of modern pattern units can be traced in some of the illustrations in the *Notes*, but generally the seventeenth- and early eighteenth-century style seems to have been elaborate, more florid and less precise than the quilts we know. Some of the patterns are so irregular that they seem to have been drawn without any help from templates and there is a good deal of free and easy "doodling." *Shell* and *diamond* backgrounds are common, *wine-glass* is found on a large scale, with *roses* and other fillings, some vague *worms*, and *feathers*, particularly in festoons.

The earliest quilts discovered in the West Country by Mrs. Hake look more like the later nineteenth-century work; a Devonshire quilt of 1750 has free and easy border-filling like some of Miss Sanderson's work, its fan corners and round centre are similar in plan, though different in detail, to patterns on many recent Welsh quilts. A Somerset quilt made in 1807 has a *running feather* of the delicate seventeenth-century type across the ends, but the rest of the pattern might be found in Wales today.

A quilt seen in Westmorland which is reputed to have been made in Northumberland in the reign of Queen Anne has a design in what is usually called the Welsh style with geometrical border and round centre, and many well-known units such as *heart, fan, leaves* and Durham *rose*. Another one, made in Pembrokeshire in 1770, resembles later Welsh work in its general arrangement, and uses familiar *leaf, fern* and flower units. Its central panel is pretty and unusual, with little stars scattered upon a background of small diamonds.

Old Joe's quilt (Fig. 11), made before 1826, is now so flat on

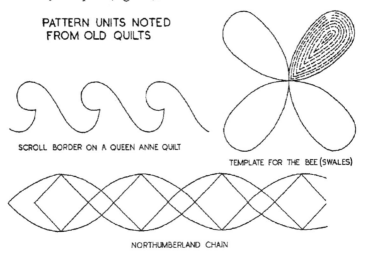

PATTERN UNITS NOTED
FROM OLD QUILTS

SCROLL BORDER ON A QUEEN ANNE QUILT

TEMPLATE FOR THE BEE (SWALES)

NORTHUMBERLAND CHAIN

its plain white side that its quilted pattern cannot be reproduced here. It combines the earlier free and easy style, with vague, sprawling flower sprays in the centre, with a rich profusion of pattern units arranged in borders in a more conventional manner.

In fact there is such a variety of styles in these few early quilts that it is impossible to generalize much about them. One can safely say that the so-called Welsh style, with borders in rectangular frames and a round centre, has been in use in many districts for some two hundred years. Many pattern units have also been in universal use for a long time. Strip-patterned quilts were probably not made before the nineteenth century, when factory production and aniline dyes brought a wide range of textiles in many colours and designs within the quilter's reach. Curiously enough, we do *not* find in early quilts what most people would call the typical traditional feather patterns, such as those shown in Figs. 47 and 54. The *running feather* (46) is certainly an old border pattern and it is natural that in the course of tradition it should be used in pairs for the centre of the quilt and have a border added. But the other style seems to have been developed comparatively recently and to have been copied and varied by so many workers that it has become the typical Durham style of the twentieth century. Whether it owes its origin to some talented designer with original ideas, or whether it can be traced back to earlier quilts as yet undiscovered, remains to be shown. The patterns which Mr. Gardiner of Allendale originated are another notable development of tradition within the last hundred years. The more geometrical style, with framed borders and round centre, which had evidently been traditional for some hundreds of years, seems to have died out in the north of England whilst continuing to flourish in South Wales.

It is a pity that we do not know the place of origin of many quilts in the Victoria and Albert Museum; with so little other evidence it is impossible to guess what were the characteristic local styles before the nineteenth century, though the similarity in general plan of several North Country and Welsh quilts of the early part of that century suggests that traditional patterns were fairly universal. Local similarities there must have been, through the natural borrowing and sharing of ideas between neighbouring craftswomen, but all the evidence indicates that the tradition was shared to a great extent by quilters all over the country. It was influenced, of course, by current fashions in design for textiles, embroidery and other decorative work, but many of the general ideas about quilt design and many of the pattern units have persisted through centuries and were probably common to quilters long before the earliest evidence which has survived.

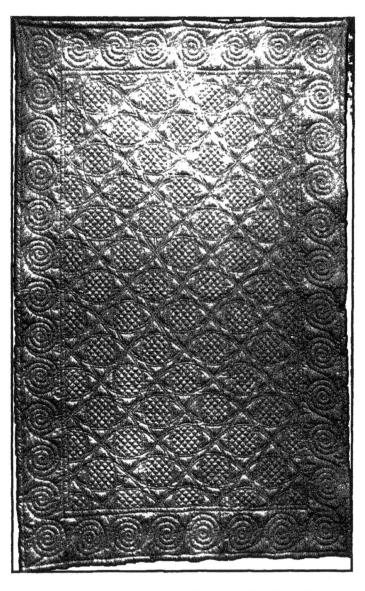

53 Small quilt by Miss Gwen Stone, Glamorgan The effective design is based on the pattern of overlapping circles which is called *wine-glass* when done on a small scale

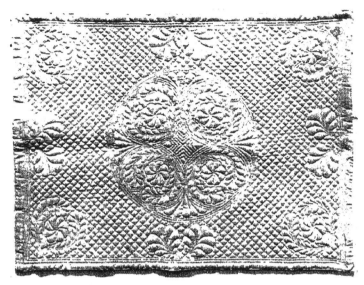

54   Cot quilt by Mrs Jenny Hitchcock, County Durham   Shell, rose and feather patterns

55   Small quilt by Miss Irene Morgan, Glamorgan   Traditional units form an original and effective centre

CHAPTER SEVEN

The Uses of Quilting

B Y the end of the eighteenth century quilted garments were no longer seen in the world of fashion; fine ladies no longer displayed a full quilted petticoat beneath an open overskirt and their cavaliers were no longer splendid in quilted waistcoats, doublets and hose (not stockings, but straight, closely fitted knickers). But not all of these things disappeared entirely; some of them merely moved down in the social scale. Petticoats or skirts, in particular, were worn throughout the nineteenth century by fisherwomen along the north-east coast, by countrywomen certainly in County Durham, Northumberland and Westmorland, and probably other counties in the North, and also in South Wales. I have heard of men's waistcoats quilted on fine black cashmere being worn in Cardiganshire and the north of Pembrokeshire, though I have not seen these.

Several Welsh quilters now living have, in their youth, quilted petticoats, usually black, of satin, merino or alpaca; Mrs. Godfrey remembered that *black* wadding was used to pad them; Mrs. Evans of Llanrhystyd knew of them interlined with flannel. Many others spoke of these petticoats—their mothers had worn them or their grannies—but for a long time I could not find one and when I asked what had happened to them I was told they had all gone underground. This was meant literally; it was the ambition of every respectable woman to be buried in a black satin quilted petticoat. A Carmarthenshire woman who used to quilt them, and who also laid out the corpses, described how these were clothed above the waist in "white cotton-wool snatched with the scissors, like flowers," and had white woollen stockings, specially knitted, on their feet. "They were going off very smart."

There are a few of these petticoats in the Welsh Folk Museum and I discovered a few more after prolonged search. The oldest ones seem to have been made (as the eighteenth-century under-skirts were) of straight widths which were put on to the waist-band in flat folds. These (and the North Country ones also) were thinly padded and sometimes quilted all the way up or, more often, to within a few inches of the waist, and some had a scalloped edge. The Welsh patterns were generally simple, there might be only *diamonds* or perhaps a border with diamonds above; but some were more elaborate; *twist, leaves, stars* and *Prince of Wales feathers* were seen on one. The village of Llangwm seems to have had its own style in petticoats of two layers of flannel, red and black, quilted together, which are said to have been worn by all the women there.

In the north of England quilted petticoats seem to have been generally worn by countrywomen up to about 1900. Some people still have them, some of the older quilters wore them in their girlhood, and many remember that their mothers made them. Mrs. Hope's mother quilted petticoats before ever she learnt to set up a large quilt in the frame; each strip of a petti-coat could be set up complete, and when, on being widowed in 1887, she formed a club and started on her first quilt she did not know how to manage a piece of work this size. Her daughter remembers with amusement how the two covers were spread out on the floor and all the padding laid in at once!

Strip patterns, such as *worm* and *twist*, were commonly used on North Country petticoats, running round them, or even plain straight lines in the same direction, or the stiff, angular *diamonds*. The idea seems to have been to emphasize the bulk of the garment rather than to attempt any suggestion of grace-fulness. Many petticoats were of white cotton; I saw a very gay one of red cotton print in the Paisley colours; homespun was the material favoured by former generations in one farmhouse; black sateen, satin or silk were also used; Mrs. Forest's mother sometimes made them from old black silk umbrellas! Mrs. English remembers that when she was a child, living in a farmhouse near Rothbury, two single women who lived together in a cottage near by wore quilted "working out" skirts of grey stuff when they were working in the fields, and a Westmorland woman said that her mother wore a skirt quilted in *diamond* pattern round the lower part. The date in both cases would be about 1900. In some photographs of fisherfolk taken at Staithes and Whitby about 1870 many of the women are wearing quilted skirts, apparently of woollen stuff, in quite elaborate patterns, which cannot be clearly seen, though a *chain* is distinguishable (7). I am told that they were worn at Cullercoats within fairly recent times (probably the first thirty years of this century) and were of navy-blue serge.

An old lady in County Durham, who quilted her own petticoats, was quilting stays for her grandchildren towards the end of the last century. One can picture these garments as similar to the quilted linen bodices of the seventeenth century in the Victoria and Albert Museum. An Elizabethan lady had a "damask quilt bodies with whalebones" and quilted night caps were in favour at that time.[1] Babies' bonnets of white cotton thinly padded have been heard of in Wales.

North Country babies slept snug under cradle quilts, made big enough to tuck in. Less was heard of these in Wales, though a Cardiganshire woman wrote that they were in use in her district as far back as the oldest inhabitant can remember, and her own grandmother "used them to bring up her family of twelve." They were usually of brightly coloured "stamp" (cotton print), sometimes with frills. In the north of England they were often of alternating strips of plain material and patchwork, or strips of print in two colours, such as pink and lilac; a white one with the patchwork basket pattern in red and another of brick-pattern patchwork in red and cream were mentioned in Weardale. Mrs. Hitchcock's mother made them of the narrow strips of material left over from quilts. One which I saw in Yorkshire had been made originally for the

[1] *History of the English People*, by R. J. Mitchell and H. D. R. Leys. Longmans.

father of the present (elderly) owners and was later used on their cradles and finally for their dolls; it was of print patchwork quilted in a simple ring pattern.

Since about 1770 big quilts, large enough to cover a double bed, have been the chief output of traditional quilters, with petticoats and skirts probably ranking next in importance until about 1900, and cradle quilts and other small things being made only occasionally. From 1900 until about 1930 the large quilts were almost the only pieces of work to be set up in the quilting frames. When the Rural Industries Bureau began to organize a market for quilted work there was at once a demand for smaller quilts, and for cot quilts. The traditional patterns were easily adapted to single-bed quilts; even in County Durham, where the workers were inclined to keep more rigidly to a traditional formula, they did not find it difficult to plan certain designs on a narrower scale—the length of the quilt was about the same as before. But cot quilts were a more awkward problem; even the memory of cradle quilts did not help much because the simple strip patterns did not appeal to London customers. The usual pattern units had to be reduced in size and the designs simplified (4, 54).

Before long these problems were solved and then cushions were demanded. Pillow-cases were certainly quilted in the seventeenth and eighteenth centuries; there is one in the Victoria and Albert Museum, which is illustrated in their *Notes on Quilting*. But they seem to have been dropped from the quilter's repertory long ago. It was the Durham workers who succeeded best with them; some of their graceful feather patterns could be arranged very effectively in a small square or rectangle and were particularly good on a round cushion; the Welsh genius for design seems to flourish better in larger spaces. It has been pointed out that to quilt a cushion cover is to misuse a craft which was primarily intended to produce a warm covering, one of the characteristic features of which is that both sides are right sides. This is quite true, but pillow covers have been quilted in the past and quilted cushion covers can be beautifully decorative. For obvious practical reasons they are popular pieces of work for beginners or for amateurs who only want to quilt for their own use or for presents to friends and may have difficulty in accommodating a large frame.

Quilted garments of more elegance than the stiff capacious petticoats of the last century came again into fashion from about 1920. Although a few orders for narrow, shaped petticoats, for long coats and evening cloaks were passed on to the quilters from wholesale dressmaking firms, these were only passing fashions, but dressing gowns or housegowns, and dressing jackets, were soon in great demand and have remained popular. Quilting is ideal for these garments, making them warm yet light (especially if a thin wool padding is used) and beautiful. The problem of how to quilt the shaped pieces in a frame which will hold only a rectangular piece of work was easily solved by chalking on the material the outline of each part of the garment and cutting it out only after the quilting was done. But the problem of designing suitable patterns for these garments was not so easily solved and there are still very few quilters who could be relied upon to do it successfully. Their grandmothers' petticoats, with their patterns running uncompromisingly around, do not help. But surely the answer is to be found in those lovely garments worn by the ladies of the eighteenth century. Although the skirts were wide and rather stiff the patterns were essentially elegant; the typical one on the scrap of Northumbrian work shown in Fig. 6 suggests a pattern of the right kind which any skilled North Country quilter could devise from her usual templates with a new one for the *rigs*. Both English and Welsh quilters have become so accustomed to designing for *quilts*, which are to be seen as a rectangular surface spread out flat, that they do not easily adjust their ideas to the quite different style of design which is to be seen, only in parts at a time, draped round the human form. For instance, pairs of wavy patterns, such as *running feathers* or *bellows*, can look quite ludicrously inappropriate; *diamonds* are rather too stiff and angular, large *roses* or *fans* look lumpy. One exquisite petticoat pattern shown in the Victoria and Albert Museum's *Notes on Quilting* (Plate 9) gives another suggestion, and there are many more petticoats in the Museum which could be studied, as well as a charming Devon one shown in two plates in Mrs. Hake's book.

The Future of Traditional Quilting

AT first glance the prospects of traditional quilting in England and Wales might seem bright. There are probably more people at the present day who have learnt to quilt and are practising the craft (though many of them may only do an occasional small piece of work) than there have been at any time since the earliest days of this century. The two areas where the tradition still lives produced in the ten years up to the outbreak of war in 1939 a quantity of quilted work which, for good sewing and fineness of design, certainly equalled and probably surpassed anything which had been done there in the preceding hundred years. The exhibition of traditional Welsh quilting held at St. Fagan's Folk Museum in 1951 showed that a considerable number of quilters are still producing work good in technique and fresh in design.

Will these present-day quilters hand on to succeeding generations their traditional knowledge ? In the past the tradition has survived through the toughest conditions. When one considers to what extent quilting became—especially in Wales —a thrift craft practised by the poor to make use of scraps of material new and old, it is astonishing that the capacity to design elaborate patterns, demanding the finest work, was still latent in the quilters. With two layers of heavy material and a padding of rags to sew through, a quilter could only do the coarsest work; even if she was lucky enough to have a length of sateen and some wool or wadding or an old blanket to work on, the small payment she earned would hardly encourage her, one might think, to do anything but a simple, widely spaced pattern. Only the spirit of craftsmanship, the feeling that it was "a lovely work," encouraged her to plan and sew the most beautiful pattern she could devise. Even the printed materials with big bold designs in strong colours, which masked so much of her work, did not dishearten her. Her love of fine workmanship and her sense of rightness in design survived all these handicaps. As soon as she was encouraged, by better payment and by critical appreciation, to do better work, she did it with delight.

The traditional quilters handed down, from generation to generation, not merely patterns as set pieces to be learnt by rote and reproduced unchanged. They handed down something infinitely more precious—the knowledge of how to *create* patterns. The method by which the new generation of quilters is taught is of great importance; if they do not learn to make their own patterns in the traditional way, always adding something of their own, the tradition will soon be dead. The technique of quilting is not very difficult; a good needlewoman can learn it quickly. But the ability to make a design which is good in itself and suitable to the work in hand is becoming rare in modern civilization. In the old days the craftsman was his own designer; nowadays people tend to think of a designer as an expert who has learned to draw, someone apart from the craftsman.

The teaching of quilting at home, by a mother to her daughter, is nearly extinct; the learner today is generally a member of a class, it may be a class organized by the local education authority in the quilting districts, or a short course arranged by the women's institutes organization, when a traditional quilter comes outside her own area to teach for a week or two. The girl who learnt at home from mother or grannie, helping her at the frame, was taught as part of the craft the planning and marking of the design. It is not so easy for the quilter in charge of a large class to teach her pupils to design their own work, especially when some of them may be only too ready to take the easy way, and let the teacher mark the whole pattern on the material for them. Some of them may be middle-aged women who never learnt to draw and think they cannot draw. A Durham woman who has taught many classes once told me that the middle-aged pupils are the most timid at designing. Perhaps the older ones remember the time when one did not, as a matter of course, buy a mass-produced pattern for any and every piece of work; the younger ones are easily persuaded that they can learn this as they have learnt other hand work; but those in between are afraid that this unfamiliar adventure may be too difficult for them and that they may make fools of themselves.

If the teacher is one of the older generation of quilters, who learnt at home in the traditional way, she knows that if her pupils do not learn to design they will not have learnt to quilt. With the use of paper templates—each learner cutting her own —and the yarn needle or a sharp-edged piece of tailor's chalk for marking, they will soon find that it is not so difficult as they had feared to mark the pattern outlines and then fill in the details. In this way they will learn a great deal more than a technique; they will learn to co-ordinate hand and eye, to draw and to stitch firm, purposeful lines and, gradually, to give expression to their own ideas; to look at a piece of work as a space to be filled, to think out how they would like to fill it, to adapt old shapes and to devise new ones, and to plan the pattern so that it is satisfactory because it is right.

In the North there are at least two enthusiasts passing on the tradition in this way; one, in Northumberland, told me recently that she has two classes in which all the learners design their own work and one double-bed and three single-bed quilts are being made, as well as cot quilts and dressing jackets. The other, in Weardale, has many young girls and young women in her classes and all learn to design.

But the ideal method of teaching is not always followed. Through lack of time for the teacher to help every member of a large class effectively (some L.E.A. classes in South Wales are far too large; thirty is not an unusual number of members)— through the pupils' own lack of enterprise, sometimes through the teacher's own incompetence, learners may finish a course without having attempted even to mark their own patterns, much less to design them. They may only have achieved small pieces of work, such as cushion covers and dressing jackets, and

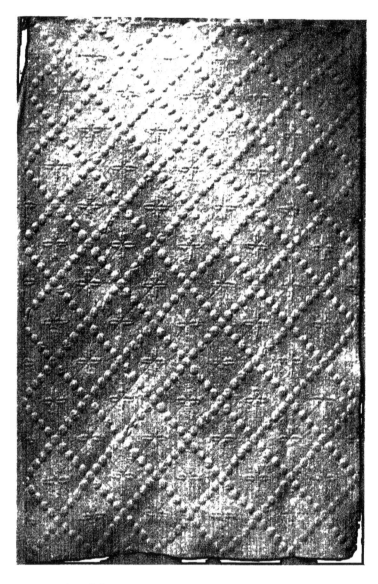

56 Small quilt by Miss Emiah Jones, Carmarthenshire. The pennies and crank patterns stand out against a background so closely quilted that it looks stippled

57 Quilt by Mrs Muriel Davies, Carmarthenshire The original design
shows the influence of Miss Emiah Jones, her teacher. It is comparable in
style to the eighteenth-century work shown in Fig. 10

thus have failed to learn how to set up a full-sized quilt in the frame. Classes are sometimes held in schoolrooms full of desks where there is no space for big frames and not even the possibility of standing a number of small ones on suitably firm supports.

A Welshwoman, when asked about some original features in the design of a handsome and well-sewn quilt which she was showing, replied that "it was marked by my teacher in chalk and I don't know any other patterns." A good Northumberland quilter told me that her classes only work on cushion covers and similar small things and "they don't want to mark their own patterns," so she does it all for them. These instances show that the mere fact that every year dozens of classes in so-called traditional quilting are held does not mean that the tradition is being carried on. The very popularity of the craft may be its misfortune because it attracts people who regard it merely as a kind of fancy work, who have no interest in tradition, who are content to quilt one or two small pieces of work under guidance and will then turn their attention perhaps to barbola or lampshades.

Many of the quilters in County Durham who were doing such good work between 1920 and 1930 were elderly women; some are now dead and others have put away their frames for good because of age and infirmity. It is disheartening to hear how few of their daughters are quilting. Again and again the story is that "none of my daughters would learn" or "one of my daughters learnt but she never does it now." In South Wales a number of younger women, who learnt the craft thoroughly in the classes organized by the Rural Industries Bureau, are still doing excellent work; but under modern conditions it is not likely that many of them will teach their daughters to quilt. In fact the tradition, handed down until now in the family, must depend for its future life upon the method of class teaching.

Classes are not confined to the districts in which traditional quilting still flourishes. Teachers from County Durham and Northumberland and, less often, from South Wales may go far afield, for visits of a week or so, and when the course is finished the learners may be left in the air. If they can only set up a small piece of work and quilt it along the lines of a pattern already marked for them, how are they to start on something new? They will certainly never be able to pass on anything of value to others. A class of this kind might well be a starting point for enquiry about surviving traces of a local tradition and quilts made a few generations ago. But the teacher, proud of her own county's prowesss in the craft and unwilling to admit that any other county could equal it, ignores this opportunity. For instance, classes in "Durham quilting" have been held for Women's Institute members in Westmorland without any reference to local work, although there are known to be many old quilts in the county, and in the office of the county federation of W.I. there is even a collection of Westmorland templates. If these, and some old quilts, had been brought out for discussion and comparison the members of the class might have been set on the way to studying their own local tradition, devising new templates and developing their own local style, instead of merely copying that of a neighbouring county.

Quilting may long continue to be practised and taught as a craft, the well-known pattern units (many of them already recorded in various publications) may still be used, but this will not necessarily mean that the vital creative spark will survive. There is real danger that the tradition may go the way of so many other traditions; not to be entirely lost, but to cease to live and grow. That is why I have attempted to collect the traditional knowledge and put it on record. It is a dangerous thing to do, involving the risk of stereotyping it, so that it becomes a set of rigid formulae. Therefore I have tried not to dogmatize about what is the "right way" but to note as many as possible of the different ways of marking patterns and working them and to set down as much as possible in the words of those who know. I have not neglected any evidence I could find, even when it shattered a previously formed theory, and I hope that this record may encourage others to search out old quilts and further information with an enquiring mind. I believe that traditional quilting must have survived, especially in remote villages and farmhouses, well into the nineteenth century in districts where it has not yet been searched for, and that old people could still talk of it and old quilts still be found. Perhaps some of those quilted skirts worn by fisherwomen on the northeast coast are still packed away in mothballs in their descendants' cottages; perhaps the forerunners of the modern "Durham feather patterns" are lying safe but forgotten in attics, maybe in Yorkshire.

Is there any real value in traditional knowledge which makes it worth some effort to keep it alive? Quilts may be preserved in our homes and our museums, patterns may be recorded in photographs, the technique may be exactly described in the written word and by illustrations. What more is there? There is the skill to go on creating new patterns. The records are something from the past; they have an antiquarian and perhaps an artistic interest, but the tradition has an educational and psychological value. If the new generation of quilters are taught in the traditional way they will have learnt much more than to make pretty things for their homes and even perhaps to earn a few pounds by making them for others. They will have learnt to co-ordinate hand and eye, to "see" the pattern in their minds, to draw the outlines and to sew even the unmarked lines accurately and rhythmically. They will have acquired a sense of design which can make their bare stretch of material flower into patterns; they will be able to see ideas for patterns in the everyday things around them—a flower, a leaf, wickerwork, ironwork or woodwork—and will find much entertainment in devising a new template. And all this adds up to the satisfaction derived from creative work, from expressing one's own ideas and making something peculiarly one's own.

A Durham woman told me how she was "very low in her mind" after her husband's sudden death, followed by other misfortunes; she could take no interest in life until she decided to get out her quilting frame. In spite of her unhappiness she was soon absorbed in the old fascination of "studying what to put on" and then "seeing the patterns form under her hand." "The quilting saved my mind," she said. This stimulating effect of an occupation which can completely absorb the powers of the mind for the time being is not peculiar to quilting; any artist or true craftsman knows it. But when so much "handi-craft" is done with all the materials ready-made, ready-drawn, ready-cut, in fact so "ready" that the *mind* is hardly occupied by the process at all, any work which demands creative effort from the worker is worthy of preservation. The quilting tradition is a skill from the living past which remains alive, enabling the quilter of today to create new beauty. It is in her hands, and in the hands of all who teach quilting, to see that it is passed on alive to the future.

References to Quilting from the Fifteenth
to the Eighteenth Century

I AM indebted to Mrs. Hake, author of *English Quilting Old and New*, for the following references, which she has come across in the course of her reading and kindly allows me to use.

Fifteenth century. In *Tudor Cornwall* by A. L. Rowse (Jonathan Cape, 1941), Chapter III: "Industry: Trade: Shipping," we read that "a typical return cargo from Britanny [to Padstow] was that of the *Julian* of St. Brieuc, bringing 200 pieces of linen, 300 of canvas, 3 bolts of canvas, 3 pieces of checker ray and one quilt valued at 3s. 4d." This was in the year 1498–99, when "innumerable little boats" came from Breton ports with their mixed cargoes of bay salt, linen, cloth and canvas, to take away Cornish fish, tin and hides. As to the cost of this quilt which was sent, no one now knows why, with the canvas and linen, and separately valued, it was about the amount of a week's wage for a working man, since tin miners' wages are recorded as low as 4d. a day and as high as 8d.

Seventeenth century. R. W. Symonds in an article "The Craft of the Coffer and Trunk Maker in the 17th Century" in *The Connoisseur*, March 1942, says that the interiors of drawers intended for linen and ladies' apparel, and the interiors of coffers and trunks, were lined with silk quilted and perfumed, and he quotes a number of upholsterers' bills in the Royal Wardrobe accounts which mention such quilted work. But it is clear from the mention of "quilt nayles" and a "bagg of Downe" that this work was not the traditional stitched quilting, but a lining puffed out with down and fastened with nails to give it the appearance of quilting.

Eighteenth century. In *Lady Nithsdale and Her Family*, by
Henrietta Tayler (Lindsay Drummond Ltd., 1939), part of a
letter written on May 6th, 1716, by Lady Nithsdale to Major
Maxwell of Carruchan is printed, in which she asks him to
supervise the sale of some of her household goods. Certain
things which she obviously valued were not to be sold, but
sent to her sister-in-law at Traquair House. Amongst them are:
"the burow, the feather bed belonging to my Lady Dowager's
bed, and the best of the other feather beds; the quilts, that is
two of them, the little one belonging to the silk dressing room,
and the cleanest of the big ones."

In *The Russells in Bloomsbury, 1669–1771*, by Gladys Scott
Thomson (Jonathan Cape, 1940), quilts occur several times in
inventories, bills and letters. "The earliest instance of an
engraved bill sent in to that family came from a firm where,
in the year 1701, the young Duchess of Bedford bought, or
had bought for her, Indian calico quilts. . . . Another bill
[which] came considerably later . . . was an account for
hose, shoes and quilted petticoats from James Cutt, coat
seller at the Ape on Horseback in Henrietta Street, Covent
Garden." The elaborately engraved bill head of Francis Flower,
Haberdasher, at the Rose and Woolpack the Corner of
King Street in Holborn, states that he "Draws all sorts of
Patterns," and one may guess that this would include patterns
for quilting.

Sarah, Duchess of Marlborough, wrote to Lady John Russell
in 1732 as follows. "But what I apprehend most, and which is
the chief reason of my writing to you, is that the bed won't be
finished time enough to have the room thoroughly cleaned and
dry to be rubbed before you come to town. And if you come
into a room that is but just washed you will get a cold, which
will be very troublesome to you at this time. I do not doubt but
that you will take care not to lie upon a new feather bed and
to have all quilts well aired."

"One entry (writes Miss Thomson, of certain accounts)
speaks of lighter things. There was a raffle—an early use of the
word in that sense—in Southampton House, for which [the
Duchess] at least took a ticket."

"May 1. 1721.   Paid Mrs. Putts Her Grace's share of a
                raffle for a quilt at Southampton House
                per order   .   .   .   .   . £3 3s. od."

The quilt must have been a costly one, but that is not
surprising in a household where brocades and velvet were
bought at 25s. and 27s. a yard—enormous prices in those days.

An inventory of the contents of "The Yellow Nursery" in
1711 includes "one Tristram quilt, 3 blankets and a calico
quilt." The first was probably quilted in a pictorial design (not
uncommon in the seventeenth century) of scenes from the
popular romance of Tristram.

Other bedroom inventories usually include quilts. For instance in the third quarter of the century:

"Clerk of the Kitchen's Bed Chamber.
    "A four post bedstead with blue morine furniture
    A feather bed, bolster and pillow.
    A check flock mattress, three blankets and a linen quilt."

"Kitchen Maids' Room.
    "A four post bedstead with green haratteen furniture; a feather bed,
    bolster and two pillows; three blankets, a rug and a lindsey back
    quilt."

An inventory taken in 1771 includes:

"Her Grace's Bed Chamber.
    "Bed.—A double headed couch bed covered with blue mixed damask,
    double brass nailed, with a dome canopy over ditto and a Gothoroon
    [*sic*] cornice
    Two feather bolsters, two check and one white flock mattresses;
    four blankets, a counterpane same as bed lined with tammy; a
    small white silk quilt."

And finally, in one of the lumber rooms, "amid the usual
jumble of old feather beds, old flock mattresses, broken chairs
. . . and the like, were many pieces which spoke of past
glories." These included:

    "Four white damask curtains
    A slip of crimson satin embroidered with silk.
    A quilt lined with red lutestring.
    Four crimson silk damask cushions."

In Sarah Farly's *Bristol Journal* an entry for Feb. 4, 1786, mentions "All the Household furniture, plate, linen and China, of a gentleman going to reside in London—consisting of mahogany fluted Four-post, Field, and other Bedsteads, with cotton, morine, check and other Furniture; Feather and Mill-puff Beds, Blankets, Quilts and cotton Counterpanes."

Ffrancis G. Payne, M.A., F.S.A., Assistant Keeper of the Welsh Folk Museum, St. Fagan's Castle, has kindly supplied the following references to quilts in old inventories.

1551. From an inventory of household stuff of Edward, last feudal baron of Powys, at Powys Castle, Montgomery:

"In the New Chamber over ye Garden
 . . . Item a qwylte of redd sylke.

In the Nursery
 . . . Item, a fether bed, a bowater, a qwylte, and a coverlet of dornes.

The Inventory of my Rayment
 . . . Item, a quylte dowblet of changeable color, taffata."

From *Mont. Coll.*, Vol. 18, pp 344–54.

1592. From an inventory of the goods of Sir John Perrot, Carew Castle, Pembrokeshire.

"Item ij old quiltes of yellowe sercnet, xx s
Item a changeable silke quilt, price xx s.
Item an old black and white silke quilt for a bedd, price iij s."

From *Arch Camb.*, Vol XII, 3rd series, pp 339–44.

1584. From an inventory of the goods of John Stapleton, Llanbrynmair, Montgomery·

"In the P'rlor
 . . . vj quiltinges."

From *Mont. Coll.*, Vol 23, p. 287.

1683. From an inventory of the contents of Wynnstay:

"Over ye old parlor & passages
 . . . 1 quilt bed and matt

Over the drawing roome
 . . . 1 quilt bed and matt

Over the butry and hall
 . . . 1 quilt bed

The old parlor
    . . 1 new quilte bed and one old one
Furniture in the gatehouse
In ye Roome over ye last menconed roome [1 e the chamber]
    . . . 1 quilt bed"
                                    From *Arch. Camb.*, Vol. XCV, pp. 49–52.

1673. From a bill from John Thomas, Salop, to Sir Mathew
Price, Bart., Newtown, Montgomery:

    "2 quilted capes 1 leyne   .   .   .   . o. 2. 8"
                                    From *Mont. Coll.*, Vol. 32, p. 77.

c.1742. From an inventory of household stuff of Robert
Jones of Plas Brith:

    "In the room above the kitchen
        a quilted chair."

1710. From an inventory of goods of William Wogan of
Llanstinan, Pembrokeshire:

"In the House . . .
Room over Cedar Room
    . . old quilt . . .
Oak Room
    . . . quilt . . .
Great Parlour
    . . couch, quilt with pillows . . ."
                            From *West Wales Historical Records*, Vol XIV, pp. 225–6.

1744. From a household account of Lady Lisburne, Brynog,
Vale of Aeron, Cardiganshire:

    "Paid for quilting   .   .   . 2s. od."
                            From *West Wales Historical Records*, Vol. V, p. 295.

AUTHOR'S NOTE.—It is reasonable to guess that this sum was
paid for making a full-sized bed quilt, since the payment for
this about a hundred and fifty years later was still only four
shillings and sixpence or five shillings.

These scattered references show that quilted work, particularly for bed furniture, was in common use throughout these
centuries.

157

Old Joe, the Northumberland Quilter,

circa 1745-1825

T HE following article, which appeared in the *Hexham Courant* of January 7th, 1947, and the accompanying extract from Hodgson's *History of Northumberland*, are reprinted by the courtesy of the Editor of that paper, who supplied copies of both.

JOE THE QUILTER—THE UNSOLVED WARDEN MURDER MYSTERY

Until the year 1872 there stood on the road between Warden Church and the village of Chollerford, overlooking the North Tyne, a little cottage. Low wall, a thatched roof and with crazy gables, it would have served well as the witch's cottage in *Hansel and Gretel* and for long it bore as fell a reputation.

For within its walls greed, the lust for gold, and a sudden, killing passion were let loose. An old man was battered to death, and his murderers are unknown to this day.

The victim was one, Joseph Hedley, known at the time of his death, and for years before, as "Joe the quilter." Seventy-six years old, he was honest, so far as is known, and kindly, and he had a reputation of being wealthy beyond the dreams of avarice. That reputation probably cost him his life.

His father decided that Joe should be a tailor, but fate had other ideas—and so had Joe. He had talent—a talent for designing and making quilts. He made hundreds of them and they were "sure fire" hit with the local housewives of the time. For years after Joe had squared his last account, the products of his needle graced the beds of many homes in Hexham and its not so immediate neighbourhood.

"Let a man make a better coat than his neighbour, and the world will beat a path to his door," runs the old adage. Well, Joe's murderers beat a path, a bloody one, to his door, but before that the quilter's fame and his products had travelled half across the world, to America, and thus was born the ideal legend of the old man's wealth.

In his quiet Warden cottage he was wont to entertain of an evening the wandering gypsy and itinerant pedlars of the times, and from this fraternity Joe gleaned his wide and peculiar knowledge of happenings up and down the country which he would retail when in the mood, with rare gusto. It was indeed a pedlar, a woman, among the last to see Joe on the night of his murder, when he was taking supper with a friend, and the woman knocked on his door and asked to be directed to Fourstones.

Ever gallant, Joe gave directions—and said that had he been a younger man he would have accompanied the lady thither.

The lady departed on her way, as did Joe's supper guest, and when the quilter was seen again, four days later, when alarmed neighbours forced in the locked door, Joe was a corpse, and a grim looking one at that.

He had been beaten almost to pulp and the weapons obviously wielded by two men were a garden hoe and a coal rake. Two weapons presupposed two murderers, but even for those Joe, with all the weight of his seventy-six summers heavy upon him, was by no means "easy meat." He had fought at the door, for the door posts were blood-spattered and had grey hairs—Joe's hairs—adhering to them, while the little living room looked as if a tornado had passed through it. The furniture was broken, a heavy clock was lying in fragments, while the bed tester had been violently torn down. Plates and crockery on the table were drenched with blood, which had seeped through the table-cloth and left an indelible stain on the wood, and in the next room lay Joe, battered and lifeless.

The hue and cry was raised, a reward was announced by the Secretary of State, Sir Robert Peel, who actually offered a free pardon to anyone, even if implicated, who would give information about a crime which was a nine days' wonder in the district.

Nothing happened. Joe the quilter's murderers had come out of the night, and back into the night they went, never again to emerge, so far as their identification was concerned.

One of the strangest aspects of a strange and terrible tale is the fact that more than one person passed and re-passed the cottage in which Joe lay still in death, between the Tuesday night early in the year 1826 on which the crime was committed, and the following Saturday, when the cottage door was forced open, yet never a one thought to investigate the fact that the front door was closed and a pair of clogs stood outside. That door was never closed while Joe was "in residence."

The murderers had carefully obscured the window of the room in which Joe was found—a disused lumber room—but the fact that the window was shrouded seemed to have struck no one as peculiar. From the mud on Joe's clothing it was assumed that he had broken away from his assailants and had made a break for safety, but was dragged back to the cottage.

The imprints of his two hands, one on each doorpost, were found—imprints stained with blood—from which it is probable that he clutched the posts in a vain effort to prevent himself from being dragged into the room, where the life was finally beaten out of him. His reputation for wealth had proved his undoing and his murder remained unsolved to this day.

His quilts kept his memory green for many a day and many a good housewife would say to envious neighbours, "this is one of Joe's quilts. You remember, he was murdered by none knows whom," and she would look anew at the work of Joe's honest hands, as if in those careful and exquisitely neat stitches the mystery of his death could be read. . . .

An unsolved murder. There have been many such, and will perhaps be many more. Quilts that travelled over half the world and a grim, creepy cottage remain the only memorials to the crime, and even they went their way as time's inexorable grasp closed on them. With the pulling down of the cottage went the last local link with Joe the quilter.

Why was Joe killed? There is little doubt that his reputation for wealth had become known, and had attracted wandering vagrants as the lure for easy money has attracted others since and led them, too, to deeds of blood and violence.

Or was it a personal feud, an ancient enemy or enemies finding vengeance as man has ever found it since the first murderer slew his brother?

Unlikely. All the records speak of the old man being loved and well respected in the Hexham district. No, it was murder for gain this old-time deed of blood, and the fact that it was futile so far as "booty" went was of little comfort to the victim.

Now Joe is only a memory, a page or two in the records of the Time and Place. But his story has been worth re-telling.

From Hodgson's "History of Northumberland":

1825 (January 3rd). A murder was committed upon the body of Joseph Hedley, a highly respectable man, better known in the neighbourhood by the name "Joe the quilter" than by his own. He was a solitary widower, eighty years old, residing in a cottage in Homer's Lane, near Warden, Northumberland, and living partly on alms and partly still by his own industry.

> "His quilts with country fame was crowned
> So neatly stitched, and all the ground
> Adorned with flowers or figured round"

that his assistance in this branch of art, as well as his entertaining and lively company, was much sought after by all the neighbourhood; and his cottage and adjoining garden were models of neatness. He was known too, at times, to grace his board with some four silver table spoons and two silver salts; and his tea table with silver spoons; and all this decency of appearance, and a constant flow of good and kind feeling, while they made him widely beloved, excited some envious calumniator to spread abroad a report that he was wealthy, and this became seduction to the cupidity and cruelty of another too powerful to resist. His cottage, body and clothing, when his mangled remains were found, retaining convincing proofs that he had made a brave and powerful struggle to save his life. The murderer remains undetected.

APPENDIX III

Quilters' Earnings

NORTH OF ENGLAND

Date	Payment for Work on a Quilt	
c. 1890	1s. 6d. to 2s.	for marking pattern, two marked in a day.
	10s to 15s.	an old lady at Guisborough, Yorks, living on parish relief and earnings from quilting and shirt making
	5s.	for re-covering an old quilt (same worker)— "there wasn't much pattern on that!"
1900	5s.	W Auckland, Co. Durham, quoted as a low rate for rough, simple work; one made in a week.
	about 15s. to 18s.	Weardale; a sateen quilt, sold for 30s.
1900–14	about 40s. to 50s	Miss Sanderson, Allendale, thought to be silk quilts for special order
	25s.	Miss Humble, Weardale; very fine work
1914–18	8s. to 10s.	Co. Durham, for a local shop
1920–30	15s.	Co. Durham
1927	30s.	Weardale.
1952	about 40s.	Northumberland; two workers, selling their quilts for from £6 to £8 10s.
	45s. to 60s	
	100s.	for an unusually large quilt, 3 yards square, Co Durham

Date	Club Quilts sold for		Approx. Min. Cost of Materials
1890	30s.	or more with a frill. Cleveland, Yorks.	10s.
1900	28s. to 40s	(special) for chapel club, Co. Durham.	15s.
	24s.		

Date	Club Quilts sold for		Approx. Min. Cost of Materials
1912	28s.	closely stitched but careless, Co. Durham.	
c. 1914	30s.		
1917	50s.	two made in a fortnight, three working.	20s.
1920	70s.	Amble, Northumberland.	
1920–40	60s.	Tweedmouth Made in three weeks	35s.
	50s.	Co. Durham.	
up to 1930	22s.	Co. Durham.	
1927	110s.	Co. Durham; very good worker.	80s.
up to 1940	30s. or 35s	with frill Made in two weeks	

SOUTH WALES

Date	Payment for Work on a Quilt	
Up to 1900	4s. 6d. to 5s.	Several informants. Speed varied from one a week to one a fortnight.
1900–10	5s.	Carmarthenshire. Good worker.
	5s.	for plain *diamonds* ⎱ Carmarthenshire.
	10s. to 15s.	for patterns ⎰
1907	5s. to 12s.	averaging 8s. on twenty-six quilts made in a year; Aberdare. The cheaper ones had 1″ or 1¼″ *diamonds* and zigzag border.
1914	10s.	
	10s	with plain edge ⎱ Carmarthenshire.
	15s	with scalloped edge ⎰
1914–18	15s	Carmarthenshire.
1917	42s.	is said to have been paid in one instance in Cards., but possibly this was the *price of the quilt.*
1920–30	10s. 6d.	Pembrokeshire; good work.
	15s	for "piecing together" and quilting, Pembs. Rough patchwork and crude quilting.
	20s	Carmarthenshire.
1920–39	15s. to 20s	for clubs in the mining valleys; seven to ten days to make; rough work.
	18s.	for an Aberystwyth shop.

Date	Payment for Work on a Quilt	
1940	28s.	charged for a silk quilt made for a Manchester customer, who sent additional payment of 20s. on seeing the work
	15s to 20s	Carmarthenshire (one who had charged 5s. when she started work in 1890)
1949	25s.	Glamorgan. Four to five days to make; simple pattern but good work.

NOTE —The quilts are of double-bed size 2¼ by 2¼ yards was the standard measurement in South Wales, and the North Country ones are of similar size, sometimes bigger

From these figures the usual rates of weekly earnings of the village quilter, selling her work to farmers' or miners' wives, can be estimated as follows.

pre-1900	WALES:	2s. 6d. to 5s. (professional full-time quilter).
	NORTH:	5s. (one instance only and considered exceptionally low).
1900–14	WALES.	4s to 7s. 6d.
	NORTH:	7s 6d. to 10s.
1918–30	WALES:	5s. to 10s
	NORTH·	7s. 6d to 15s.
1930–40	WALES:	9s. to 20s.
	NORTH·	10s. to 15s
1950–52	WALES:	25s to 30s.
	NORTH:	20s. to 40s.

When the quilter was paid an exceptionally high sum for a special order she would doubtless put a great deal more work into it, so her weekly earnings were not much larger

These earnings may reasonably be compared with the wages of agricultural labourers in the same districts; though these were notoriously low in the earlier part of the period under review, they look like wealth beside the quilters' earnings; certainly the labourer usually had to support a family, but he had many allowances in addition to his cash wages and his wife and children might also be earning something by field work. In South Wales from about 1880 to 1898 a farm worker's cash wages might be as low as 10s. weekly but the usual rates were from 15s. to 20s. In the North they were about 17s. By 1913 they averaged 18s 1d. in South Wales and 24s. 8d. in Durham and Northumberland. By 1918 30s. to 45s. was paid in County Durham; slightly less in Northumberland.

INDEX

The numerals in heavy type refer to the *figure numbers* of the illustrations

Lightning Source UK Ltd.
Milton Keynes UK
UKHW010753221122
412637UK00009B/445

9 780343 300524